DEVOTIONS
FROM THE
BARN DOOR

Also by Tammy Chandler

Devotions from Everyday Things
More Devotions from Everyday Things
More Devotions from Everyday Things: Horse & Farm Edition
More Devotions from Everyday Jobs
More Devotions from Everyday Sports

with David Weill
Deployed with my Mother

DEVOTIONS
FROM THE
BARN DOOR

TAMMY CHANDLER

WordCrafts

Devotions from the Barn Door
Copyright © 2023
Tammy Chandler

ISBN: 978-1-957344-89-8

Published by WordCrafts Press
Cody, Wyoming 82414
www.wordcrafts.net

CONTENTS

FOREWORD

In my third book, I wrote about my horse journey from riding my aunt's Morgan horse at four years old, to my daughter owning her own horse and being her glorified groom, and my husband gifting me a one-in-a-million horse for Christmas. Life has moved into new seasons for our family—all three of our children are grown and married, and the older two are having children of their own. The farmhouse is an empty nest, but everyone comes and goes and fills the house again with laughter. We've been touched by sorrow, sickness, joys, and new life. We have found that this journey is best traveled with Jesus leading the way and family and friends alongside, and this book is a reflection of the lessons learned during this season of my life. I hope you will join me as we explore the farm for deep spiritual truths that show up among everyday things.

I am humbled once again that our heavenly Father saw fit to allow me to see the everyday lessons and to share them with you. I do not take it lightly that you chose this book—thank you. I look forward to exploring the barnyard with you, and I am praying for you. Enjoy the view.

PREFACE

D*evotions from the Barn Door* is the sixth book of the *Devotions from Everyday Things* series. Each book in the series is a devotional in which you will find spiritual truths connected with ordinary things. It's a straightforward approach toward helping us on our journey to find deeper spiritual truths in the world around us. *Devotions from the Barn Door* connects with the lives and objects of farm life.

How to use this book: The devotions are quiet times with God based on lessons we can learn from the farm. Each one contains a daily Scripture passage, an illustration from the barnyard, a Thought-provoker, and a Prayer Starter. The Scripture passage allows us to see the connection to God's Word; the illustration will help us apply the principles of Scripture to something we can take with us throughout the day. The Thought-provoker is an opportunity to adjust our thinking or actions to the principles learned from the devotions; it is also a Journal prompt if you prefer to write your thoughts. The Prayer Starter is a conversation starter about the topic of that day's devotion. It is an opportunity to thank God for what we are learning, and to ask Him for the strength we need to apply new Biblical principles to our hearts and lives. It is also a time for us to share our burdens and pour out our hearts about personal struggles we are facing, and express our joy and thanks for the good things He does as we go through each day.

Thank you for joining me for this journey through farm life in *Devotions from the Barn Door*. I am humbled and excited that you have chosen this book, and I am praying for us to know God in a deeper, richer way because of our time together. Let's get started.

THE BARN DOOR

I am the door. If anyone enters by Me, he will be saved, and will go in and out and find pasture.

John 10:9

Those who live the farm life know that it is a busy life. There are crops to tend, animals to feed, repairs that need to be made, equipment that needs maintenance—the list never stops. We have chores to do, manure to move, seeds to plant, life to live. All of this crazy, wonderful life centers around the barn, at least it does here at our farm. We travel in and out of the barn door several times a day, but do we really stop to notice it? The door that provides protection from the elements, keeps out unwanted critters, and opens each morning to a new day. We hear the squeak of the hinges and the sliders as we crack it open each day and shut it each night—but do we truly see what the barn door is? What it stands for? How it stands?

Maybe your barn door is older and sagging some, but it still does its job. Maybe you are a new generation farmer, and your door is brand new. Or maybe you are somewhere in the middle. Your barn isn't new, but it doesn't feel worn out yet. Take a moment to study the door.

For that is where this journey begins. The next sixty days will be about spiritual lessons we can learn from the farm, and that journey begins with faith in the Door. Jesus calls Himself the Door, and by entering into a faith-love relationship with Him, we are saved, and we will go in and out.

As we traverse the farm life over the next sixty days, we will view it from the barn door. We are going to find lessons in the barn, in the pasture, and all around the barn. But we start with the door. I hope you know the Door, personally, as your Savior, but if you don't, please take a moment to study Him. Stand in awe of His strength, His character, and most of all, His love. His love for you—He loved you so much that He could not picture eternity without you. So, He paid the price for your sin and mine, and He offers salvation. Salvation from sin, from yourself, from never being good enough. He has taken all of that for you—just walk through into a new life with Him, your Door. Then, swing the door wide and tell everyone you know of how He changed you.

Thought-provoker:

Have we each walked through faith into a love relationship with Jesus Christ, our Door? Take a moment to tell your Door story to someone today.

Dear Lord, thank You that You are the Door that leads us to salvation through faith. Help us not to forget all You did to secure a love relationship with us and eternity forever. Help us see You for Who You Truly are, our Savior and Lord. In Jesus' name, Amen.

NOTES/INSIGHTS:

Sunshine

"Then all this assembly shall know that the LORD does not save with sword and spear; for the battle is the LORD's, and He will give you into our hands." So it was, when the Philistine arose and came and drew near to meet David, that David hurried and ran toward the army to meet the Philistine.

1 Samuel 17:47–4

Sunshine is a miniature donkey who came to us as a package deal with another horse. She is an adorable miniature—a stereotypical donkey with long ears, an Eeyore-like tail, and a bit of a stubborn streak.

Being a donkey also has another interesting trait—donkeys do not speak horse. By this I mean that horses have a routine, they have an order in the herd, they live by habit. There is a certain order as to who eats where, and who gets to the food first.

They have an order when it comes to going out to pasture, coming in at night, and the list goes on. Sunshine disrupts all of this. If she wants to go out first, she runs and puts herself at the front of the line. If she sees a pile of hay or a scoop of feed she wants, she snorts, kicks up a bit, and makes a scene to protect the pile from any other horse who may have a thought of taking it from her. When it comes to people, Sunshine will do whatever it takes to get her ears scratched first. She loves to be out in front, and she will take on a horse twice her size to prove it.

David had a little bit of Sunshine's attitude. When he got to the battle where his older brothers were, he heard a giant defy the armies of the living God, and he did not care that the giant was at least twice his size; he knew, by God's power, it was time to take him down. While all the others had developed a habit of fear and hiding, David went first. He put his confidence in the God he knew, and he stepped out. When all was said and done, the giant was dead, the enemy defeated, and others were encouraged by David's courage and confidence in God.

I think David would have liked our Sunshine. I think he would have seen that her stubbornness is more a sense of confidence and steadfastness. She knows who she is, but her size doesn't matter. She is willing to buck the habit of fear, break the normal order of things, and fight for what she wants. We need to be like Sunshine.

Buck the fear. Have courage, and stand up for the things you know God wants in your life. Speak donkey in a world full of horses.

THOUGHT-PROVOKER:

In what areas of life is God asking us to buck fear and stand up?

Dear Lord, thank You that when You are for us, no one can be against us. Help us to stand in that confidence today and to buck the fear we see around us. In Jesus' name, Amen.

NOTES/INSIGHTS:

THE RESCUED HORSE

For though by this time you ought to be teachers, you need
someone to teach you again the first principles of the oracles
of God; and you have come to need milk and not solid food.
Hebrews 5:12

When my friend Kristi rescued Charlie, he needed help. He had been starving, and every rib, vertebrae, and pelvic bone was showing through his thin coat. He had a very sweet demeanor, but his body was in serious need of nourishment, and he had several hundred pounds to gain. He was in his teens and should have been enjoying the prime of his life. Instead, he stood here in front of me with imploring eyes and a weak frame.

We started by feeding him mash—a mixture of beet pulp and other nutrients that would be easy on his digestive system and restart his metabolism. He sniffed it at first, then, he tasted it, and his interest perked up. Over the next several weeks, Charlie received bucket after bucket of mash, and as he kept at it, we started adding more and more of the grains and carbohydrates he needed to be able to keep up with the others in his pasture.

It took a year, but Charlie gained the weight—because my

friend knew he needed to be fed, and he needed a new environment to thrive and become the horse we knew he was on the inside.

So many Christians today are like Charlie. They encountered Christ at some point—accepted His gift of grace and redemption, and then they stopped eating. They walked away from the spiritual nourishment that comes from a regular encounter with the Bread of Life through the words He left us in the Scriptures. And, at some point, someone else sees them starving. They encourage them to get back into the Word with accountability and a new environment of community within a small group, Sunday school class, or church family. Little by little, the starving one starts to feed on the Word again. They start to gain new strength. They start to relearn principles of Scripture that they knew before, and they start to gain the weight of Biblical knowledge and obedience in their lives. When they should be actively involved in the work of the body—evangelism, discipleship—they are relearning how to walk themselves.

Charlie never looked back. Once he knew he was in a safe place with an owner who loved him and met his needs, he started to eat. He gained weight, and now this sixteen-hand, fully fleshed out Saddlebred cross with the blond mane and blaze is a beautiful picture of health. He is strong and steady, and he eats every chance he gets. When it comes to spiritual nourishment, stop starving. Start eating. Be like Charlie.

THOUGHT-PROVOKER:

Are we spending time in the Word and nourishing our souls, or are we starving ourselves?

Dear Lord, thank You for the banquet You provide each day

in Your Word. Help us to stop starving ourselves and to feed our souls in Your Word each day. Help us to grow every time we open it up. In Jesus' name, Amen.

Notes/Insights:

GREEN BEAN PICKING

For the word of God is living and powerful, and sharper
than any two-edged sword, piercing even to the division of
soul and spirit, and of joints and marrow, and is a discerner
of the thoughts and intents of the heart.

Hebrews 4:12

Part of living on a farm, at least for me, is having a summer garden. I love picking fresh vegetables and putting them up to enjoy in the winter. Green beans are especially enjoyable to pick, as they present a challenge. The vines and leaves grow very thick, in order to protect the beans, and so I have to reach in and find the beans. Some beans are easy to pick—they are hanging right at the edge of the vines, and they are easy to pull off. Others are deeper in the undergrowth, and I have to reach in and pull harder to retrieve them. And some, are in the very back of the vine and I have to pull apart the twisted vines and reach all the way in to find them and then tug hard to get them to come off the vine so we can enjoy them at the dinner table.

Studying the Scriptures is similar to picking green beans. Sometimes, we can spend just a few minutes and find a bean of truth that helps us through the day. Other times, we have to dig a little deeper in order to find a stronger truth that takes us time to tug on and really understand. And then there are times when the meaning of a certain passage is so deep that it takes a lot of effort to untangle the vines and really grasp the meaning of a deep truth that transforms our mindset or drastically changes our behavior.

I am grateful that the Lord allows for all three different types of studying in His Word. Sometimes, I need a simple truth that encourages and builds me up and allows me to go on with my day, but other times, I need the deeper truths of God's Word that transform my thinking and cause change in my behavior. And then there are the days in between, where He reassures me of His love, gives me a nugget to learn from His Word, and allows me to see that I need to continue to learn and grow. If we didn't have the easy picks, we might get discouraged and not continue to pursue truth. If we didn't have the deep studies, our souls might yearn for more. God in His great wisdom gives us exactly what we need from His Word and satisfies us with good things, just like green beans at dinner time.

THOUGHT PROVOKER:

Are we doing all three types of Bible study so that we are encouraged, growing, and really digging into God's Word? Which type of Bible study do we need to focus on today?

Dear Lord, thank You that Your Word is so approachable, so rich and so deep so we find all we need for our spiritual journeys. Help us to study Your Word in many different ways, so that we find all the treasures You have for us. In Jesus' name, Amen.

NOTES/INSIGHTS:

Margaret

For there is no distinction between Jew and Greek, for the same Lord over all is rich to all who call upon Him. For whoever calls on the name of the Lord shall be saved.

Romans 10:12–13

We have a wild turkey that hangs out at our farm. She is a lone turkey, and she stays with the horses in the pasture. She might even think she is a horse, because she would rather be in the pasture with the horses than in the hay field with other turkeys. Although she is wild, we decided to call her Margaret. Margaret doesn't look like a horse. She is a wild turkey with a bald head and long dark feathers. She has two legs, not four. She does not neigh, she gobbles, and she sleeps in the tree by the barn, not in a stall. And yet, the herd has accepted her and is keeping watch over her when she is around. She walks out to the pasture with them. They allow her to eat with them, stand in the shade of the trees, and even drink from their water trough.

Margaret reminds me that there are members of the family of God who do not look like me. We sponsor two boys in different countries, and though they do not look like me with their dark eyes and deeper toned skin, they are still family. Our sponsored sons are across the world, but Margaret reminds me that different lives across the street and across town too, and God calls us to accept them into His family. We are not all going to be the same, but we are all accepted by the same Father, and we are all family.

Margaret challenges me to remember that God the Father does not have biases, and I am to follow His example. God loves all people, right where they are and just how they are. When God brings a Margaret into my life, I need to be like the horses—accept her as part of our herd—to welcome her in and make her feel accepted. And I need to remember, sometimes, I am the Margaret. Sometimes, we are the ones who do not look like the rest, and we are so thankful when we are accepted and loved. We need to remember that God's family is based on blood—His—and not what we look like or how different we are. We all are on the same footing because we all have been bought by the same blood.

THOUGHT-PROVOKER:

Where is God challenging us to love those who are different from us? Where can we engage today to share the love of Jesus with anyone, everyone, along our journey?

Dear Lord, thank You that You have no biases, but that everyone is welcome into Your family by the blood of Your Son. Help me today to accept and love those who are different from me, and accept the love and grace from them as well, because that is what You would do. In Jesus' name, Amen.

Notes/Insights:

Lola

Brethren, join in following my example, and note those who so walk, as you have us for a pattern.

Philippians 3:17

Lola was a sweet horse. She came to us for the last few years of her life, and although she had arthritis and had to stop carrying riders, she was still the leader of the herd until her final days. She was an alpha mare who had taught hundreds of kids the love of horseback riding and made sure that the horses in her herd stayed in line. They all respected her and learned from her. When a new horse came to the farm, Lola did an amazing job of acclimating them to the herd.

There was one horse, Gus, who came to the farm for a short time. Gus did not have a lot of training, and he was very strong headed. Lola gave him some space for a few days, but there came a time when she was done with his stubbornness. She led Gus to the edge of the pasture one day, and as I watched, she stomped her front foot, whinnied a deep warning, and backed him up. She repeated the process three times, and the third time, Gus got the message. He dropped his head, whinnied submissively, and followed her back to the herd. From then on, Gus got his instructions from Lola, and he learned how to behave with other members of the herd.

There are members of the church family who are like Lola, and there are some who are like Gus.

The Lolas are the seasoned members of the faith who have journeyed far. They have taught others by their example, and they are respected among the believers. They do not have to be harsh or unkind, but they do know what the Word says about how we are to live and be among the unbelievers in the world. They are usually tolerant of younger, immature believers, just like Lola gave Gus time and space to figure some things out when he was new in the herd. But there also comes a time when these seasoned believers come alongside a new believer, teach them principles from the Word and guide them to help them become better members of God's herd.

Lola is remembered for her gentleness and her leadership. She taught many young people to love horses, and she taught horses how to be good ones. Lola's legacy is one of kindness, patience, and strength. May we be remembered the same as we lead others into the herd of God, and then walk alongside them and help find their place among the members. May others see us as the kind, seasoned defenders of the faith who are helpful and willing to take time to help and guide as others grow.

THOUGHT-PROVOKER:

Are those of us who are seasoned in our faith helping others to grow and become good members of the herd? Are we encouraging them to be a part, or are we pushing them away? For those who are newer in our faith, are we willing to listen to the wisdom and guidance that comes from good mentors?

Dear Lord, thank You for the mentors You have placed in our lives to help us be better, stronger, and mature in our faith. Help us to listen to them and learn from them with respect and love. And help those of us You have called to be mentors to be gracious, kind, and loving as we guide others to grow in You. In Jesus' name, Amen.

Notes/Insights:

Pawing at the Door

And He said to them, "Go into all the world and preach the gospel to every creature."

Mark 16:15

W e have two horses in the barn that have a good, bad habit. By good, I mean that it gives a great example of how we should live our lives, but bad, because—well, pawing at a stall door is not something that we promote as a good habit at our barn.

Every morning, though, right after they have eaten breakfast, the two of them start. It's as if they know they have been fed, and now it is time to get out into the world and do what they were called to do. They paw at their stall doors, loudly requesting that the door be opened for them to get on with their day. As soon as the doors are opened, they stroll out to the pasture and accept their responsibility of being a horse and a donkey for the day.

The lesson I have learned from the two of them is how amazing it would be if each one of us who follow Christ would eat our spiritual breakfast of quiet time with Him in prayer and in the Word, and then be *loudly determined* to get out into the world and do what He has called us to do. If we were pawing at the door of our prayer closet, just asking God to release us into our neighborhoods, communities, and even the world, to be the light and love that He has called us to be, we really could change the world.

Sadly, I think there are many of us on many days that would rather stay in that closet instead of getting out into the messy world. After all, when the horses get out in the pasture after it has rained, they sometimes get muddy—very muddy. The world can be a messy place when we get out and share the Gospel. Some might not want to hear it, others may mock it, still others need it more than we could ever imagine.

It is time, at least for me—and I hope for you too—that we start pawing at the door after our spiritual breakfast and get out into the world where we are meant to be, doing His work, for His honor and glory. Staying cooped up just makes us restless and stiff. Getting out there makes us trust Him more, is good for our hearts to grow stronger in love, and our witness to be bold in His grace. Let's start pawing at the door.

THOUGHT-PROVOKER:

Are we eager to get out in the world and fulfill the Great Commission, or would we rather stay inside the stall of comfort? Where do we need to move today to be where He wants us to be?

Father, please help us today to be excited about the opportunities that You have for us to get out into the world and fulfill Your commands to share the Gospel and to love. Help us move out in Your strength today and leave the stall of comfort behind for a world that needs You. In Jesus' name, Amen.

Notes/Insights:

THE RUN-TO

He calms the storm.

Psalm 107:29a

We recently had storm damage at our farm. No worries—all the animals and humans were safe, but the run-to that the horses use for shelter from the sun, wind, and rain was uprooted and flipped over. I was out at the barn working when it happened, so I saw the run-to flip over. This outbuilding, a three-walled, roofed shelter that was supposed to provide protection, went up in the air and was flipped over on its roof by the wind. I saw it happen, but there was nothing I could do. The straight-line winds were stronger than the shelter, and over it went.

It made me think of all the things we build in our lives to protect ourselves. We build shelters for our emotions, we build walls, we build prisons—places that were meant to protect but have actually imprisoned our hearts. Why do we do this? To protect our hearts from hurt and our souls from pain.

What I realized watching that shelter go over is that our walls are no match for a storm. Our shelters are pitiful in the face of life's great winds. We need to find our refuge in the God who calms the storms, not in a shelter that still feels all the winds and rain when the storms come. God is the only refuge that will stand when the storms come. He is our Rock and our Redeemer; He is our Refuge (Psalm 18).

After the storm was over, my husband got the tractor out, we called some friends, and we turned the run-to back over. The roof is damaged and there are repairs that need to be made, so it stands as a reminder that God is the only refuge that can stand against anything this world throws at us. Anything we try to build to protect our hearts has the potential to be toppled when the storms come. Better to find refuge with the One who calms the storms. Hope you find yourself under the shadow of His mighty wing today.

THOUGHT-PROVOKER:

Are we trying to find shelter in our own contraptions today, or are we running to the Rock who is greater than all?

Dear Lord, please help us see that our attempts to shelter ourselves from the storms of life are only going to blow away and topple over. Today, let us find our refuge in You, the One who not only shelters us, but You also calm the storm for us. You are so good! Thank You for Your never-failing, never-ending faithfulness. In Jesus' name, Amen.

NOTES/INSIGHTS:

THE LONE HORSE

"What do you think? If a man has a hundred sheep, and one of them goes astray, does he not leave the ninety-nine and go to the mountains to seek the one that is straying? And if he should find it, assuredly, I say to you, he rejoices more over that sheep than over the ninety-nine that did not go astray."
Matthew 18:12–13

We have a horse that no matter who is calling for dinner, no matter if the entire herd has come in to eat, we have to go get her. For some reason, she thinks the grass out in the field is better than the grain we give, and she thinks she can manage alone in the dark. We have to trudge out to wherever she is, throw a rope around her neck, and lead her in.

Many of us are like that lone horse. The Lord has prepared a bountiful, spiritual spread for us to enjoy at His table, but we still won't come. We stay out in the fields of the world and think the wild, worldly grass will somehow satisfy our souls. We ignore His invitations to come and join the family of God at His table, and we keep as far away as we can from being taken in. But the night is coming, and the Good Shepherd knows the time is short, and so He willingly comes after us. He doesn't trudge. He keeps drawing closer and closer, calling our names and inviting us to accept His offer of salvation. The offer He made the day He died on Calvary and then rose again three days later, to prove He was the Only One who could truly save our souls and bring us into the fold.

If you are out there, in that worldly pasture today, thinking that the wild grasses are going to satisfy your soul, stop staying away. Stop resisting the invitation to come in for dinner with the family of God. Stop ignoring the Savior's call and just allow Him to throw the rope of surrender around your neck and follow Him. He promises a life of love, joy, and peace, because of His presence. Your soul will find what it is truly seeking in a Shepherd Who laid down His life for His sheep.

Tired of being the lone horse? Tell Him. Ask Him to bring you in from the wild pastures and to feed your soul with His redemption. Tell Him you know you don't deserve it, you don't measure up, but you know He paid the price for you, and you are tired of running outside the boundaries of His love. He will take you in, and you will find peace with the Savior. The lone horse can become the loved horse—just come into His herd.

THOUGHT PROVOKER:

Are you the lone horse, or the loved horse? Are you in God's paddock?

Dear Lord, thank You for being willing to chase down a lone horse like each of us to show us Your love and to share Your salvation with us. In Jesus' name, Amen.

NOTES/INSIGHTS:

STONES

When Jesus had raised Himself up and saw no one but the woman, He said to her, "Woman, where are those accusers of yours? Has no one condemned you?" She said, "No one, Lord." And Jesus said to her, "Neither do I condemn you; go and sin no more."

John 8:10–11

There are rocks everywhere around where we live. If we are putting in fence posts, we have to dig up rock. When we trail ride, we go over and around rocks. Some are in the ground; some are sticking up out of it. Some are so big we need equipment to move them. Others are small enough that they fit in the palm of a hand. They are all hard and feel permanent.

In our story, the leaders brought stones with them. Those stones were hard and were planned to be used as a permanent solution to sin. Once she was dead, there was no going back. They would use the law to justify their actions, and they were ready to trap God Himself with their tactics.

Jesus had other plans. His solution was grace. Grace supersedes stones. Man wants sin wiped out—and the sinner taken with it—grace separates the two. Jesus went to the cross to wipe away the sin, but He keeps the sinner intact. Jesus shows that love is superior to the law, not because we don't need the law, but because the law destroys the sinner as well; we need His love to keep us from death.

Grace also comes with a new directive: go and sin no more. Now that her life had been rescued by grace, she couldn't keep living the same way she had before. She was to go and be different. Some say "sin no more" is impossible, but it wasn't impossible for this woman to stay out of adultery. He didn't tell her "Go and be perfect," He told her to walk away from her old life and live such that people knew she had found grace. She stepped out of the darkness and into His Light, which is the verse that follows this story (see John 8:12). She doesn't get to stay the way she was; grace made her shed those sins and walk in the newness of His Light.

We are all "that woman" before Christ intervenes, covers our sins with His blood, and gives us a new direction when we accept what He did for us through faith. We need to live differently because of the grace He extends to us. Stones remind us that human methods are hard—we prefer to take out the sinner with the sin. Grace separates sinners to a new way of living.

Thought-provoker:

Where do we see God's grace extended in our lives today? How do we need to live differently so others see that grace?

Dear Lord, we are so grateful for Your grace that separates the sinner from the sin and gives us the opportunity to go and sin no more! Help us to live so differently because of the grace You have extended to us. We love You and thank You that grace supersedes stones. In Jesus' name, Amen.

Notes/Insights:

WAFFLES

But as for you, speak the things which are proper for sound doctrine: that the older men be sober, reverent, temperate, sound in faith, in love, in patience; the older women likewise, that they be reverent in behavior, not slanderers, not given to much wine, teachers of good things—that they admonish the young women to love their husbands, to love their children, to be discreet, chaste, homemakers, good, obedient to their own husbands, that the word of God may not be blasphemed.
Titus 2:1–5

W affles is my oldest hen. She has been with me for seven years, and she was about two when I got her. This is a very old lady in chicken years! She can no longer lay eggs, but she is a wonderful matriarch in the flock. I have introduced three sets of young pullets into the flock during her years and each young hen was graciously taught by Waffles. She teaches the young ones to hunt worms, to find treats in the grass, to hide from hawks, and to find shelter during the storms. She is not aggressive, she is patient as she leads by coming alongside. She eats with them, spends time with them, and they, in turn, respect her and follow her lead.

Titus encourages older Christians to be the *Waffles* in their circles of influence. He admonishes them to set a good example, be grounded in their faith, and teach good things. Teach the younger ones how to hunt the Scriptures for answers to their life questions and desires. Teach them to find shelter in prayer and encouragement when the enemy flies overhead. Teach them to run to their true Refuge in Jesus Christ when the storms of life come. Just like Waffles, mature Christians need to be patient and not aggressive. Hen-pecking does little to promote sound Biblical truths and obedience to God's principles. Most hens avoid hen-peckers, and young Christians will too.

If you are a mature Christian, be willing to spend time with the younger ones. Waffles spends hours upon hours with the younger hens. They learn from her, but they also enjoy being with her. And she enjoys them as well. I think Waffles stays young at heart because of all the time she spends with the younger hens. And I think the younger hens become wiser and safer from all the time they spend with Waffles. Together, they all make for a healthy flock of chickens.

Thought-provoker:

Do you see in your life where you are like Waffles to others? Are there others who have invested in you? Have you shown your gratefulness to them for the time they have spent with you? Are you willing to commit to spending time with someone else for the good of God's flock?

Dear Lord, thank You for Waffles—someone who comes alongside and leads us closer to You and Your ways in love, not out of obligation. Help us to see who we can touch with this kind of love today. In Jesus' name, Amen.

Notes/Insights:

MUD

What shall we say then? Shall we continue in sin that grace may abound? Certainly not! How shall we who died to sin live any longer in it?

Romans 6:1–2

One thing is inevitable on the farm: rain makes mud. While I am always grateful for the rain that helps the grass, flowers, gardens, and fields to grow, I have to be careful about my attitude toward the mud.

When we first started farming, I would just plow through the mud. It was everywhere, so I thought the best way to deal with it was to just get ankle deep and struggle my way through it. Sometimes, the mud was so thick my boots would get stuck, and my foot would slip out of one, and I'd be hopping around trying not to fall and get my foot back in my boot without getting my sock gross and soggy. I would have to wash my boots off again and again, and my jeans kept getting dirty from the mud splashing up on them as I trudged through the mud.

A few years into farming, a friend of mine made a comment that changed my whole view. "Why don't you watch where you step?" was all she said. Made a lot of sense, once I stopped and thought about it. If I were more careful where I stepped, I wouldn't have to deal with so much mud aftermath. I started picking my way carefully through the paddocks and barn lots. I noticed my boots and jeans didn't get so dirty, my boots stopped sticking in the mud, and my jeans weren't getting stained anymore.

Mud on the farm can be a lot like sin. It's everywhere—all around us in the world. In fact, Paul said that if we were to stay away from all the sin in the unbelieving world, God would have to take us out of this world (I Corinthians 5:9–13). But should we just trudge through the sin-mud in this world and let it get all over us? I think we know the answer to that. No. We need to start taking my friend's advice and watching where we step. We don't keep plowing through the mud, trudging ankle deep and splashing it everywhere, and then hoping the hose of forgiveness will get the mud off. Instead, we grow in grace by watching where we step. We don't go to those places where we know we are tempted to sin—whether it's a physical location or a place in our own minds. We show grace changed us by living differently.

Today, we need to show that grace has affected us, God's grace has changed us, by watching where we step.

THOUGHT-PROVOKER:

In what ways are we still trudging in the mud of sin? Where do we need to apply grace by changing where we step?

Dear Lord, thank You that grace means we aren't stuck in the mud because of Your sacrifice and forgiveness. But, today, help us grow in Your grace and refuse to trudge back into the mud by watching where we step. In Jesus' name, Amen.

NOTES/INSIGHTS:

THE MANURE PILE

Brethren, I do not count myself to have apprehended; but one thing I do, forgetting those things which are behind and reaching forward to those things which are ahead, I press toward the goal for the prize of the upward call of God in Christ Jesus.

Philippians 3:13–14

I spend a lot of time picking up manure. Each horse has the potential of leaving forty to fifty pounds of poop behind per day, so there is a lot of it to pick up. Each time I scoop up the manure, I throw it into a wheelbarrow and haul it down the hill to the compost pile. A compost pile is an amazing natural process, and an interesting thing happens there. If you leave the manure there, don't touch it, and let the heat and sunshine do its work—eventually it becomes good dirt that can be used to grow things again. Manure, by itself, is too potent and too acidic to be good for growing plants. It stinks, and it cannot be used for anything in its moist state. But compost the manure and it becomes a wonderful mixture of nutrients and organics that help plants to grow healthy and strong.

Our achievements in life are a lot like that manure pile.

On their own, they are too potent with pride to help things grow in our lives. When we brag about them, it can become stinky to others, and our hearts get full of useless thoughts of how important we think we are. But when we leave our accomplishments alone (forget them, so to speak) and allow the Lord to work on them through the heat of trials and the sunshine of humility, they become the fertile ground in which new spiritual growth can occur in our lives. When we realize our past accomplishments were only by His will and for His glory, then we build confidence in our God and His abilities, not our own. As the acid of self gets absorbed and changed into service and concern for others, we are able to grow patience, gentleness, meekness, faith, and other fruits that come from depending on the Spirit as we continue to achieve and accomplish. And because the acid of pride has been removed by the heat of trial and the work of humility, it won't burn up the good things growing in our lives. We will see the Lord get the glory for the growth instead of wasting our efforts trying to get man's praise (Matthew 6).

Thought-provoker:

Where do we need to pile up our pride, forget it, and let our accomplishments become fertile soil for more good works? Are there areas in our lives today that need the heat to help make them fertile again?

Dear Lord, thank You for humility and compost. Thank You that You can take the manure of our human pride and turn our hearts into fertile ground that can grow things for Your honor and glory. Help us to learn to trust Your process. In Jesus' name, Amen.

NOTES/INSIGHTS:

JULIO

I, therefore, the prisoner of the Lord, beseech you to walk worthy of the calling with which you were called, with all lowliness and gentleness, with longsuffering, bearing with one another in love, endeavoring to keep the unity of the Spirit in the bond of peace.

Ephesians 4:1–3

Julio is my one in a million horse. When I was managing a barn before we moved to our farm, he was the shy horse who had reverted back into the herd after his owner had passed away. As I worked at the barn and he got used to seeing me, we all noticed that he started following me around. Long story short, the barn owner talked with my husband, and Julio was my Christmas present those many days ago.

Julio is a true beta horse. He is not pushy, he doesn't demand to be at the front of the herd, and he waits patiently at the gate as the other horses pace back and forth, positioning themselves to get in first at feeding time. He literally hangs back and waits until the way is clear, and then he heads to his stall. It is a true picture of gentleness and longsuffering. Julio's ways are so opposite of the typical herd horse mentality. He has learned that he has less stress and receives less aggressive behavior from others. He has become quite content to be the gentlemen at the back of the pack.

Julio's actions are an example of what we should be as we walk through this life. The world says be pushy—be assertive—to get ahead. Others tell us that we can't hang back or we will be behind. Julio has learned the secret. When we walk the way laid out in the Word of God, we can relax, knowing God has our journey, our successes, and our failures, in the palm of His hand. Julio doesn't have to be aggressive, because he knows his provision is waiting for him in his stall. God does the same thing for His people. Psalm 23 tells us He prepares a place for us, even when our enemies are looking on. We can rest in the fact that we are His children, just as Julio rests in the idea that he is my horse. He doesn't have to jockey for a position, worry about standing his ground, or being aggressive toward other horses because he is secure in who he is with me. We can be the same with our Savior. He asks us to be humble, gentle, and longsuffering. We can trust that this is the best way because it is His.

THOUGHT-PROVOKER:

Are we being pushy and aggressive, thinking that will help us get ahead, or are we willing to live out the principles in God's Word, even when they are opposite of the world?

Dear Lord, thank You that we can relax because You have everything under control and because You have asked us to live in humility, gentleness, and longsuffering to show the world Your ways are different, and so much better. In Jesus' name, Amen.

NOTES/INSIGHTS:

City Folks

Now these are the ones sown among thorns; they are the ones who hear the word, and the cares of this world, the deceitfulness of riches, and the desires for other things entering in choke the word, and it becomes unfruitful.

Mark 4:18–19

W e have some very dear friends who live in the city. They come out and visit us at the farm on occasion, and we love to have them here. They don their blue jeans and cowboy boots, take up an accent—we don't think we have one, but they do— and they will talk "farm." They want to help with chores, but they are not sure which instrument is a pitchfork or a muck shovel. We gently guide them, and they have a blast—for the week they are here. They look like they could be farmers, they do their best to talk like farmers, and they live the life—for a week.

But then they go back to their city home. They swap their blue jeans and cowboy boots for suits and dress shoes, and they head back to their *real* jobs in the city. They soon lose the accent, and there is no need to talk farm vocabulary around city people, so they change back to city talk, and while the farm visit is a great memory, it doesn't fit in the lives they are currently living in the city.

I think of this example when I read today's passage. Jesus is talking about sowing seed (sharing the Gospel), and the seed falls into different types of soil. There are some hearts that are so hard, they won't even entertain the idea that they need a Savior of their souls. In the parable, the birds come and snatch the seed off these wayside hearts before it ever has a chance to take root. Other seed fell on stony ground, and this is where the city folk example hits home. This soil wants the seed, but there are so many other things distracting them that the seed takes root for a little bit, but then they go right back to the things that make their hearts stony. Jesus explains that cares of this world, deceitful riches, and desires for other things choke the Word. Just like the city life deems that our friends don't wear their farm clothes, look like farmers, or talk like them, there are people who suffer from stony hearts keeping the Word from taking root.

I'm glad the parable doesn't end there; it would be very discouraging. The final ground is good soil. The seed germinates, and it produces fruit. This would be like our friends moving from the city and becoming farmers full time. That sure would be something!

Thought-provoker:

Are we living our Christ following as a once-a-week trip to the farm, or are we living daily and producing spiritual fruit like permanent farmers?

Dear Lord, thank You for the reminder to be full-time farmers with good soil that produces Spirit-fruit, and not just living for You for a week, or only on the weekends. In Jesus' name, Amen.

NOTES/INSIGHTS:

THE BARN LIGHT

Then Jesus spoke to them again, saying, "I am the light of the world. He who follows Me shall not walk in darkness, but have the light of life."

John 8:12

Right above my head at the barn door is a big, barn light. The light is steady, strong, and bright. When it gets dark, I am very grateful for that light. That light deters coyotes and other predatory animals from coming close—they avoid being seen in the light, and that keeps the horses safe. That light also provides guidance to the barn when the horses have to be put up late, or if I need to go drop extra hay at night during the cold winters.

Recently, that light bulb blew, and it became pitch black around the barn. I was nervous walking up to the barn because I couldn't see what was ahead of me. I noticed the coyotes howl got closer that night, and the horses were spookier than usual when we brought them to the barn for the night. Thankfully, a ladder and a replacement bulb—and a husband willing to climb up there to change it—solved the problem, and the light shines brightly again as it should.

I am grateful that Jesus said He is the Light and His Light will never go out—He is the same, yesterday, today, and forever (Hebrews 13:8). When we walk in the Light in our lives by staying in His Word and being a reflection of Him, the enemy—the soul predator—has to stay away, and others benefit from the peace and safety He provides for us by His presence. The barn light stays on in the dark, but I have to be close to it to benefit from the protection and illumination it gives.

The light also gives the horses comfort and helps to keep them calm as they come to the barn in the dark. So it is when we walk with Jesus—the closer we walk with Him, the brighter His Word and His Light shines in us, guides us, and protects us. It also benefits others as we are able to reflect that light and be confident as we walk through the dark by being focused on the light and all it provides.

I don't know about you, but with all the darkness there is in the world, I am glad to walk in the light with the God who knows and who cares all about us. It's so good to know that He knows where we need to be, and He lights the way.

THOUGHT-PROVOKER:

Are we walking in the Light, walking with Jesus, or is there something keeping us from the light? May God show us what needs to change so we can walk in the Light today.

Dear Lord, please help us to walk in the Light of You and Your Word this day. Help us see that staying focused on You keeps the enemy from coming in, and we find our peace by being where we are supposed to be—close to You. In Jesus' name, Amen.

NOTES/INSIGHTS:

THE WHINY BRAY

Do all things without complaining and disputing, that you
may become blameless and harmless, children of God with-
out fault in the midst of a crooked and perverse generation,
among whom you shine as lights in the world.
Philippians 2:14–15

Sunshine is a very sweet donkey, but she has an issue: she has
a whiny bray. She doesn't always use it. Most of the time, she
brays happily from the pasture or the paddock when she sees
someone coming, and she swishes her tail and perks her ears
up as she lets a happy bray curl from her lips. But her whiny
bray is different. She pins her ears back, drops her tail and lets
out a long, annoying bray that reaches a fever pitch if someone
does not respond to it quickly. She usually uses this bray when
she is not getting something she wants. If she is hungry and it's
taking too long to scoop her feed. Or if she is hot and wants
cold water put in her bucket. It's a demanding, whiny bray that
grates on nerves and makes her seem petty and annoying. When
Sunshine uses this bray, most people want to distance themselves
from her, and the other horses seem to be annoyed by it too.

God tells us to do *everything* without complaining or disputing (arguing). Complaining makes us sound like the world, God says that not complaining makes us sound like His children. When we can hold our tongues in difficult situations, when we don't complain, whine or argue when things don't go our way, or don't happen as quickly as we would like them to, we shine as lights in the world. And that light goes a long way to quelling the darkness of discouragement and defeat around us.

I am trying to teach Sunshine not to use the whiny bray. She gets rewarded when she waits patiently for her food or water and doesn't whine. She gets extra scratches between her ears when she uses her happy bray, and she gets treats when she is happy around others. God says that we become blameless and harmless children of God when we don't complain. Peace and protection are added rewards of not complaining. I hope we all can try—maybe for just one day—not to complain. And then I hope we will determine to try each day after that.

Compliments will go so much farther than complaints, and we have the added benefit of being like our heavenly Father when we choose not to complain.

THOUGHT-PROVOKER:

How very hard it is to not complain, but what a difference it makes! How will we catch ourselves today and make the effort to compliment instead of complaining? How can we change our mindsets to one of compliments?

Dear Lord, thank You for the great challenge to compliment instead of complaining. You know this goes against the very nature that many of us default to, so please help us to be overcomes today and to make a bright light with compliments in the world around us. In Jesus' name, Amen.

Notes/Insights:

THE GUNSHOT

That we should no longer be children, tossed to and fro and carried about with every wind of doctrine, by the trickery of men, in the cunning craftiness of deceitful plotting, but, speaking the truth in love, may grow up in all things into Him who is the head—Christ.

Ephesians 4:14–15

There is a target range not too far from our farm. Most of the time, we hear faint shooting sounds as most of the people using the target range are using small ammunition. Every once in a while, however, we hear the loud crack of a high-powered rifle or the repeated shots of an Arma Lite Rifle. These loud noises disrupt the horses' routines and they run from the back of the farmland up to the barn with their eyes wide and their nostrils flaring. They buck and kick and run from one end of the paddock to the other.

If I see them acting this way, I will make my way out to the barn and talk quietly to them. After they calm a bit, I will go in the paddock with them, gently brush their necks and rub their favorite itchy spots. I want them to learn that the eerie sounds of the loud gunshots are nothing to be afraid of—the bullets from those sounds can't touch them. There is no need for them to be so wound up about something that will not reach them.

Those gunshot sounds are a lot like the trickery of men and deceitful plotting that are spoken about in our passage today. Sin has become prevalent as people move farther away from God and do what seems right in their own eyes. Lots of evil things in our world make loud noises, but none of those are able to separate us from our Savior (Romans 8:35–39). There is no reason for the winds of the false doctrines or craftiness of men to alarm us or unsettle us in our faith. Just like the horses, we have a home that is settled, an identity that cannot be shaken in Christ. Just as my calming words help the horses to remember where they are and who they belong to, the truth of His Word shields us from being deceived.

A couple of days ago, the rifle cracked again at the range. The horses looked up, but they didn't tear off for the barn. I smiled. They are learning that their identity here on the farm gives them security, and they don't have to be unhinged by something loud and disruptive. May we be the same, secure, and confident in Christ, the One Who gave His everything for our salvation.

THOUGHT-PROVOKER:

Where are we being disrupted by the noise of false doctrines and man's deceitfulness? How can we be more secure in our identity in Christ and stay calm in loud situations?

Dear Lord, thank You that our identity is secure in You, and we do not need to be alarmed when men are deceitful in the world. Help us bring Your peace to those around us. In Jesus' name, Amen.

Notes/Insights:

THE TURTLEDOVES

Surely goodness and mercy shall follow me all the days
of my life; and I will dwell in the house of the Lord forever.
Psalm 23:6

There are two turtledoves who make their home in the tall tree right next to the barn. They enjoy eating the seeds left over in the hay stalks after the horses have their morning feeding, and they flit down to the ground and peck at seeds and pigeon-waddle their way around in the morning sunlight. They chirp quietly to each other, and they watch out for each other by taking turns keeping an eye on the barn cat to be sure he doesn't have any ideas about an early morning snack.

The two turtledoves are never far from the barn. They might light on the electric wire outside the barn front door, or they may sit on the barn roof when it's cool in the afternoon shade. Even during storms, we see them hunkered down in their nest in the tree outside the barn, their tail feathers being the only thing we can see from the ground. We hear them cooing in the early evenings, and we enjoy watching them raise a family each spring.

One of the things I find fascinating about the turtledoves is the noise that their wings make when they take off. There is a fluttering sound that no other birds make around the barn, so we know it is them, and we can track where they are based on the sound. The other thing I find amazing about these two is that they are always together. They always seem to come around when I am working outside the barn, and they always show up as a pair.

I have thought about naming them "Goodness" and "Mercy." In our passage today, goodness and mercy show up together. They are never far from us as the passage says they will follow us our entire lives and are still present even during storms and trials. Goodness and mercy are there in the mornings when we rise, and we can hear their soft coos of encouragement every evening. They raise hope in our hearts each season, and they do not leave when things get difficult.

I am so grateful that God pairs His goodness and mercy. I am thankful we see the results of their presence in every season, every turn, every trial. Knowing goodness and mercy will always be around gives us the hope that we are never lost in despair. If life is difficult, listen for the fluttering sound of the wings of goodness and mercy—they are there, paired together, and given to us as partners to lift our spirits and help us as we rise each morning and lay our heads each night.

THOUGHT-PROVOKER:

Where is there evidence of goodness and mercy in our lives today? Even in hard times, where do we hear the fluttering of wings that tells us they are still here?

Dear Lord, thank You for goodness and mercy, as they give us hope as we journey this life path. Help us hear the flutter of goodness and mercy in our lives today. In Jesus' name, Amen.

NOTES/INSIGHTS:

Rukiyah

Then He took the child by the hand, and said to her, "Talitha, cumi," which is translated, "Little girl, I say to you, arise."

Mark 5:41

Rukiyah stayed with us for a time in between jobs for her owner. She is a spirited games horse with lots of energy and a quick brain. She has great ground manners and loves to be around people. She seems to enjoy life and not take a moment for granted.

Maybe that is because she was rescued from the kill pen. Others thought she wasn't worth the time or the effort, and she wound up being as good as dead in the eyes of the horse traders. But, then…. Mercy stepped in.

A rescuer noticed her and saw something no one else did. This horse that was as good as dead, had someone breathe life back into her spirit. She walked out of that kill pen on a lead that led her to a brand-new life of hope and goodness. Her name, "Rukiyah" means "She rises up."

Rukiyah reminds me of a little girl in Scripture. She was lifeless. She literally was dead in a physical sense. Others had already started mourning her loss, and her parents were desperate. But then…. Jesus stepped in.

Her father pleaded for Jesus' help, and He came. Even when it seemed all was lost, He told them to "Believe." Jesus walks into the house, puts the mourners out, takes her by the hand and says, "Little girl, I say to you, arise." Rise up from the death that tried to hold you. Rise up to life, living and purpose.

When I feel like I have nothing to offer; when others criticize and see nothing of value, or they verbalize that they don't think I am worth their time or effort—Jesus takes me by the hand. He tells me "Arise." He says to get off that bed of discouragement, leave behind those lies, and believe you are My child. Jesus says, "Little girl, I say to you, arise."

Today, if we are struggling with our worth, if we feel like we are in the world's kill pen just awaiting the inevitable—let Jesus touch our hands. Believe Him when He says, "I say to you, arise." He has so many things planned for us that we cannot see from the kill pen moment. Rukiyah had no idea she would be a games horse with great speed, a loving owner, and a happy life to live. And, if we see someone who thinks they are worthless, struggling to have hope, touch them. Extend the love of Jesus because no one should be left in the world's kill pen. "Talitha cumi."

THOUGHT-PROVOKER:

Are we sitting in the kill pen moment of our lives? Have we accepted the love and power of Christ into our lives and taken Him at His word?

Dear Lord, thank You for "Talitha cumi." Thank You that You say to us "Arise," and we can because of what You did on the cross for us and the love You shower us with each day. In Jesus' name, Amen.

Notes/Insights:

DIXIE

His lord said to him, "Well done, good and faithful servant; you have been faithful over a few things, I will make you ruler over many things. Enter into the joy of your lord."
                                                            Matthew 5:23

When Emily first asked me about Dixie coming to the farm, I honestly hesitated for a moment. Dixie is a heeler dog, and between the donkey and another horse that just does not like dogs, and a new barn cat that wasn't too fond of dogs yet, I was concerned that Dixie would get hurt. Emily assured me that she would be responsible for Dixie and that Dixie would listen. Since I try to always be up for a new adventure, we set a date, and Dixie came out to the farm.

She was amazing. She is the most well-trained, well-behaved dog I have seen on a farm. Yes, she loves to run and play, and she will fetch almost any stick or ball you can throw, but as soon as her owner called her name, she came right to her. When the kitten was out and about and got scared by Dixie's antics, her owner simply said, "Leave it," and Dixie came right back and sat at her owner's side. When the donkey came over to investigate, Dixie ran up to the fence and sniffed noses with her. When donkey's ears went back, and she put her head down, Dixie retreated back to her owner's side and whined, hoping the donkey would change her mind, but respecting the boundaries set by her owner.

You see, Dixie loves to please Emily. She lives her life attentive to what Emily tells her, and she is quick to obey. While Dixie could be pulled in so many different directions, she keeps her attention on her owner. It may seem like little things—sit, fetch, stay, leave it—but these all add up to a very well-behaved dog.

Wouldn't it be amazing if people noticed that we are attentive to Jesus like Dixie is to Emily? If we were willing to follow Him in all the little things that seem insignificant, but those things that add up to a life surrendered to Him? What if we were faithful in the small things?

I hope one day to hear Him say, "Well done," just like Dixie hears, "Good job," from Emily. Dixie hears that because she is willing to put her attention and desire on pleasing Emily and not worrying about all the other distractions around her. I hope we can do the same when it comes to living a life that pleases Jesus.

THOUGHT-PROVOKER:

Are we attentive to Jesus and the little things He asks of us each day, or are we too distracted? Are we desiring to hear His "Good job" or are we pulled in too many different directions to be focused?

Dear Lord, please help us to be attentive like Dixie to the things that matter most to You. The small things that add up to a life lived faithfully. Help us desire to hear "Well done" from You. In Jesus' name, Amen.

Notes/Insights:

Sheep and Goats

All the nations will be gathered before Him, and He will separate them one from another, as a shepherd divides his sheep from the goats. And He will set the sheep on His right hand, but the goats on the left.

Matthew 25:32–33

Our daughter went to college to study Animal Science. She and I were out walking the other day, and she shared some interesting things about sheep and goats. Both of them are ruminant animals, which means they eat things that grow on the ground and digest them in a similar manner. They are both capable of producing milk, material—wool for sheep, cashmere for goats—and both are meat animals.

But there are several differences that she explained as we walked. Goats are browsers, they are on the hunt for whatever they can find for themselves—trees, shrubs, even weeds. Goats are stubborn. They don't want a shepherd; they even battle and head butt each other to determine which one of them is going to be in charge at the moment. Goats can be defiant. They will rear up and attempt to horn the goat wranglers. They are not easily caught, and they will wiggle and squirm fiercely to free themselves from a handlers' grip. There is even a tie-down that is used to hold a goat so it can be milked without kicking the milker!

Sheep, on the other hand, are dependent on the shepherd for safe keeping. Sheep are grazers, which means they eat what they find in front of them, they don't go off hunting for something else to eat. Sheep tend to be submissive. They don't challenge the shepherd, and they don't fight for the right to be in charge. When sheep are herded, they run in a pack and don't rear or kick. Sheep can be easily caught, and they will sit beside the shepherd, or stand still while they are milked or sheared, as long as they are not frightened. The steadier the shepherd is, the calmer the sheep are.

It is always interesting to me how God uses agriculture and the characteristics He designed into animals as examples in Scripture. Today's passage says He will separate His sheep from the goats. The goats—the stubborn ones who tried to figure out their own way to God, bucked at His Word, and refused to submit to the Great Shepherd—will be on one side. The sheep—who followed their Shepherd, accepted His redemption plan, and were willing to be caught and held by the Shepherd—will be on the other. How I pray earnestly that we will be on the sheep side when He ushers in His kingdom!

Thought-provoker:

Are we being goats, trying to fight our own way into God's family, or are we like sheep who have accepted His sacrifice for our souls and have submitted to Him?

Dear Lord, thank You for the example of the sheep and the goats. How they are similar, and yet so different. May we know You as our Great Shepherd and submit to You in this life, so we can spend eternity with You. In Jesus' name, Amen.

NOTES/INSIGHTS:

THE TRESPASSER

Then Moses returned to the Lord and said, "Oh, these people have committed a great sin, and have made for themselves a god of gold! Yet now, if You will forgive their sin—but if not, I pray, blot me out of Your book which You have written."

Exodus 32:31–32

W hat do you do about a trespasser? In our situation, a joyrider lost control, took out a fence, tore up a horse trail and then proceeded to attempt to *gun his way out* of the mess he had made. His truck, buried to the axle in mud, finally came to a stop when it hit two sapling trees. He phoned a friend, who came and made him come to the farmhouse and confess what he had done. John got the tractor from the shed, and we headed out to survey the damage.

Thankfully, no one was hurt, but the damage was widespread. The horse trails will need to be regraded and seed put down, the trees and shrubs that he wiped out with his truck will need to be cut and removed. The fence needs to be replaced, and we decided to also put boulders in front of the fence so that no one else decides to joyride into our property. And to add to it, the truck didn't belong to the driver. He had borrowed it from someone else.

So, what do you do? What did we do when we were faced with this situation where we had every right to be angry? We have three NO TRESPASSING signs posted on the fence that he went through. Our driveway has a PRIVATE DRIVE sign, and our street is a dead-end. This wasn't just someone being lost or turned around, this was someone who was joyriding and thought it would be fun to tear up an old farm.

The owner of the truck came, and we decided to let him and the driver sort out the ramifications of taking the truck on a joyride. We focused on getting the truck unstuck and off our property, took the driver's and the owner's information and sent them on their way. Maybe we should have done more; maybe we should have called law enforcement or an insurance company, but our gut told us that this was an opportunity to extend grace.

I can promise you that was not my first reaction. I was angry and upset that someone thought this was okay, and that this was going to be another repair project on our already growing spring to-do list on the farm. *But God.* I had just read the story of the Israelites rebelling against God, not being willing to follow the signs He had posted in the wilderness and mur-muring against the leadership that He had set up in Moses and Aaron. God wanted to destroy all of them, but Moses stood in the gap and asked God for mercy and grace. How many times has someone stood in the gap for me? How many times has Jesus interceded for you?

THOUGHT-PROVOKER:

Are we willing to stand in the gap for someone today? Where can we extend grace?

Dear Lord, thank You for Your grace that You extend to us each and every day. Help us to extend grace to others and stand in the gap for them as You give us opportunity. In Jesus' name, Amen.

Notes/Insights:

STELLA BELLA

Do not let your adornment be merely outward—arranging the hair, wearing gold, or putting on fine apparel—rather let it be the hidden person of the heart, with the incorruptible beauty of a gentle and quiet spirit, which is very precious in the sight of God.

1 Peter 3:3–4

With a name like Stella Bella, which means, "beautiful star," you would think she would be an exquisite model of equine beauty and feminine characteristics. But, Stella, actually is a mountain horse, with thick fur, a Roman nose, and a stocky build. She likes to roll in the mud on occasion, and more than once we have had to pull prickers and thorns out of her mane. She typically puts her ears back when you take her picture, and she really doesn't like to be judged in an arena.

Stella, however, is as steady as they come. When someone is new to riding, you put them on Stella. When one of my horse-loving friends needs a horse for their novice husband or friend, we put him on Stella. When a young person who has never ridden before wants to try out a horse, you guessed it, we put her on Stella. Why? Because Stella is gentle and quiet.

She plods along the trail and things don't rattle her. She rarely spooks at anything. She is the horse that you can trust to do what she is supposed to do—help others love horseback riding.

God knew exactly what He was doing when He made each of us, and He knew what characteristics we would need to fulfill the purpose He has for each of us. I know that I am not strikingly beautiful on the outside, and I am okay with that. You may not like to have your picture taken, and you may even have a stocky build. But how beautiful is your heart? Can others trust you to introduce them to a new faith in Christ with a calm and steady spirit? Are you approachable? Are you consistent in your journey as you plod along through this life?

Stella's heart is huge. Whatever she lacks in physical form, she more than makes up for with her spirit, which nothing, not even age, can take away from her. Your beauty comes from within, which in God's eyes is very precious. *Charm is deceitful and beauty is passing, but a woman who fears the Lord, she shall be praised.* Proverbs 31:30. Be reminded today that we are all Stella Bellas—beautiful stars—that shine from the inside. Let's let our true beauty shine in the world today.

THOUGHT-PROVOKER:

Where does our true beauty come from? Are we striving to have incorruptible beauty that comes from within, or are we only focused on the outside?

Dear Lord, thank You that You have made each of us to be beautiful from the inside out. Help us today to be that meek and quiet spirit which is very precious to You and makes us beautiful no matter what we look like on the outside. In Jesus' name, Amen.

Notes/Insights:

EQUINE MEDICINE

Now no chastening seems to be joyful for the present, but painful; nevertheless, afterward it yields the peaceable fruit of righteousness to those who have been trained by it. Therefore, strengthen the hands which hang down, and the feeble knees, and make straight paths for your feet, so that what is lame may not be dislocated, but rather be healed.

Hebrews 12:11–13

Every year in the spring, my horse needs to take some medicine. He has a sensitivity to the rabies vaccine, and because he needs the vaccine in order to travel and show, we found a solution. If we give him some Phenyl Bute the day before, the day of and the day after his vaccine, his body does not react so severely. Phenyl Bute, or "Bute" as most horse people call it, is a powder that can be sprinkled on feed and most horses don't seem to mind it. My horse is not most horses, however, and he makes life a bit difficult for those three days. We have to mix the powder with water, pour it into a syringe and then squirt it into his mouth while holding his head up so he can't spit it out. If he would just realize that the medicine was helping him, and if he would just take it as a supplement in his feed, we would not have to go through the process of getting it down his throat with a syringe.

Discipline is similar to the Bute. If we would just realize that discipline is a supplement that we need in our lives in order to build our character, we would not expend so much emotional energy fighting it. If we understood that discipline helps to keep us from reacting in ways we should not, we might accept it better.

If my horse would accept the powder in his feed, he wouldn't have to go through the effort of getting the medicine down his throat via syringe. But the medicine is important. It makes it possible for him to take a needed vaccine without having the reactions of swelling and pain. Discipline is important for us too; it is the corrective force that helps our character to develop in the will of God instead of our own. The passage today says that chastening—disciplining—is not pleasant at the moment, but it yields the peaceable fruit of righteousness. It makes us able to stand in our faith, to trust Christ, and understand that we are clothed in His righteousness. Without the medicine, my horse cannot get over the reaction and his body come back to full immunity. Without discipline, we can't move on to healing. And healing is what we want. Hopefully, we will realize the process to get there is through discipline's door.

THOUGHT-PROVOKER:

Where are we resisting to accept the work of discipline in our lives? How can we accept the process and work toward healing today?

Dear Lord, thank You that Your discipline is good for us and leads us to healing. Help us trust You and move in that direction today. In Jesus' name, Amen.

NOTES/INSIGHTS:

GUS

But I say unto you, love your enemies, bless them that curse you, do good to them that hate you, and pray for them which despitefully use you, and persecute you; That ye may be the children of your Father which is in heaven: for He makes His sun to rise on the evil and the good, and sends rain on the just and on the unjust.

Matthew 5:44–45

Gus was a buckskin horse whose owner bought him for his color, not his training. He knew how to be saddled, and he would follow a horse in front of him down a trail, but he did not know what to do on his own. His cues were non-existent, and his manners were terrible. The lady who bought him kept thinking he would get better, even after he threw her off three times, kicked two other horses, and bit someone who got too close to his chin.

But Robbie decided to take Gus in. Robbie had lots of experience with horses that didn't have good manners. She was patient and worked methodically with horses that others thought were evil. Robbie realized that many horses were the way they are because people had disrespected them or treated them like enemies.

So, Robbie went to work. Gus spent sixty days being woken

up early each morning, getting groomed, saddled, and ridden. Sometimes he responded well; other days he reverted to his bad habits. Robbie kept showing up, and she kept working with him. At the end of sixty days, she had pretty much worked the kick out of him. Robbie kept training Gus with positive cues and encouragement, correcting him when he needed it, and showing him that the boundaries of good training were for his good, as well as his rider's safety.

Another sixty days later, Gus had become adjusted well enough to go to a rodeo rider. Because of Gus's speed and strength, he worked well as a rodeo horse, and he enjoyed his new life. Gus was no longer an enemy horse; he had become a team player. All because Robbie saw something in him and was willing to invest in a horse that others thought was mean and would never amount to much.

Instead of seeing people who do not understand spiritual truths as enemies and evil, we should take on Robbie's approach. We can consistently love them, invest in their lives, and help them to come to a knowledge of God and His truths that hopefully will help them to come to trust Him. We need to give them the opportunity by changing our perception of them. God loves every single person He has created, and He wants everyone to have the opportunity to choose Him.

THOUGHT-PROVOKER:

How do we regard others that are different from us? Are we willing to invest time to give them the opportunity to come to know Him?

Dear Lord, please help us to regard no one as an enemy, but all as those You want to reach. In Jesus' name, Amen.

Notes/Insights:

Garden Picking

Through the Lord's mercies we are not consumed, because his compassions fail not. They are new every morning, great is Your faithfulness.

Lamentations 3:22–23

The garden is a great place to be in the summertime. Having worked all spring to tend and work the seedlings that grew into plants, the summertime starts to show the fruits of our hard work. The produce is growing well, there is a lot to pick, there are weeds to pull, branches to prune and sweet cherry tomatoes to pop in your mouth while working. It can also be a place of hard work. It's hot, so we are sweating, and there are some weeds that have thorns that can cut our skin and some insects that bite while we are trying to work. We can exhaust ourselves working all afternoon in the garden, and then we have to be right back at it the next day as there are new weeds to pull and new produce to pick.

Our passage today tells us that God's compassions are new every morning. No matter what yesterday held—the sting of sorrow, the joy of accomplishment, exhaustion from trials or testing—each morning God renews His compassion toward us. His mercy makes sure that the trials of life do not consume us. Maybe we have spent a season of investing, tending, and caring for others, and we are just starting to see the fruits of our labor. Or maybe we are in the midst of pruning and are exhausted from the emotional toll that life changes are taking on us. Maybe we are in the heat of trials or suffering, and we are being bitten by the enemy's attempts to discourage and defeat us.

No matter what place we find ourselves in this moment of life, His compassion will not fail us. His mercies will keep covering us, and we will make it. We can believe this because of His great faithfulness. Some days are easier than others, some days are the hardest we have ever known, but He won't fail. We need to be reminded of this. The garden reminds us that even if we picked everything we saw yesterday, there will be new fruits and vegetables to find today. Even if we pulled all the weeds, there will be new ones tomorrow. No matter what is happening in the garden of life, God will make sure we have the mercy and compassion we need to keep going. He will not allow life to consume us, but He extends His mercy. His mercy covers every failure, every sin, and His compassion tends to our hearts. Each morning we can be restored by the presence of His mercy and compassion, and we can face the day, because great is His faithfulness.

THOUGHT-PROVOKER:
Where do we see God's mercy and compassion in our lives today?

Dear Lord, thank You that You are faithful. Thank You that every morning You bestow mercy and compassion and that You promise we will not be consumed. Help us to trust You, no matter what the day brings. In Jesus' name, Amen.

NOTES/INSIGHTS:

TWO ROOSTERS

If you then, being evil, know how to give good gifts to your children, how much more will your heavenly Father give the Holy Spirit to those who ask Him!

Luke 11:13

Our daughter-in-law incubated and hatched some chicks for me, and among them were two roosters. As we watched the flock grow, both roosters developed beautiful plumes and were very attractive. They were both big, strong, and impressive. But they were very different.

One rooster, the bigger, stronger one, was very kind to his hens. He would seek out food for them, cluck to them, and protect them from danger. He led his hens with grace. The hens would follow him, and he watched over them. These hens grew large, their feathers—while not as bold and colorful as his—were pretty and shiny. These hens laid eggs regularly and lived in peace. They clucked happily, rested well, and were healthy.

The other rooster, the smaller one, was very aggressive toward the hens. He didn't look out for their welfare, in fact, he went out of his way to make their lives miserable. He wouldn't share food or treats he found them, he cawed at them instead of clucking, and if one of the hens got too close, he would pluck feathers from her head or back. These hens lived in constant fear, their feathers were disheveled or missing, their egg laying was hit or miss, and they were restless and unhappy.

God, our good, heavenly Father is so different from the evil prince of this world. God knows how to love, extend grace, and offer peace (James 1). Jesus came as the Savior to make a place for each of us in His kingdom. He promises the Holy Spirit will be with us—giving us protection, supplying our needs, and strengthening us to be healthy ambassadors for Him in this world. The devil promises misery, and he delivers. He is the father of lies, murders, and every evil imaginable (John 8:43–45). While God extends grace, the devil offers grief.

The hens had a choice. Those who followed the good rooster were safe, even though dangers are ever present about the coop. They knew their rooster would defend them, protect them, and be present for them. The other hens were not so blessed. Their rooster would allow them to be attacked, harmed, or even killed before he would even notice their plight.

So which rooster would you want to follow? It's pretty simple to see the contrast when it comes to the birds. Follow the good Father who wants to love, protect, and grace you today. The other rooster just isn't worth it.

THOUGHT-PROVOKER:

Are we following the good, good Father of love this day, or have we traded His peace for the devil's deceptions?

Dear Lord, thank You for the example of the roosters that shows a clear contrast between what You offer those who love and follow

You, and what the devil destroys. Help us to choose You today, in every way, and be examples of the love and grace You bestow when we choose to follow You. In Jesus' name, Amen.

Notes/Insights:

THE FEUDING HORSES

If it is possible, as much as depends on you, live peaceably with all men. Beloved, do not avenge yourselves, but rather give place to wrath; for it is written, "Vengeance is Mine, I will repay," says the Lord. Therefore "If your enemy is hungry, feed him; If he is thirsty, give him a drink; For in so doing you will heap coals of fire on his head." Do not be overcome by evil, but overcome evil with good.

Romans 12:18–21

We have two horses that do not get along. They both are well provided for, both have been on the farm for a long time, and both have been trained. Whenever they are close to one another, however, their ears go back, their teeth are bared, and bites and kicks have happened. They will attempt to back each other into a corner and land a hard kick to the chest or flank. They simply do not want to try to be nice to each other.

So, we made them go on a trail ride together. A long trail ride. They had to give each other room to get through the narrow trails, and they had to learn to not lash out at one another as they went. At first, we thought the idea might not work, but as time went on and the trail got longer, they settled in and stopped looking for opportunities to get on each other's nerves.

Sometimes, God does the same thing with us. Sometimes we have issues with other people, and there really isn't a reason. We are all covered under the same grace. We are all provided for by our Heavenly Father, and we all are growing and maturing in our faith. In the process of growing, God puts us with people that are different than we are, those who challenge us and may even lash out at us. He puts us on a journey together to learn how to settle into our identity in Him and trust Him as He helps us work with people who are different than us.

Our Scripture passage today gives us guidelines for dealing with people we find difficult; even people we truly dislike. He tells us to live peaceably with them, to meet their needs, to trust God's judgment, and to overcome with good. He tells us to do these things to those we deem to be enemies—those on the opposite side of our perspective. Good wins because God is good, and He knows what we need to grow in our understanding of each other in this life journey. Relax and enjoy the trail ride—He puts us with those who need to help us become more like Him.

THOUGHT-PROVOKER:

Are there those on our life journeys that challenge us? Are we living in peace or turmoil—with them, and within ourselves? What can He change in us today?

Dear Lord, help us live at peace and be peace seekers. Thank You that You overcame evil with good, and You can help us to do the same. In Jesus' name, Amen.

NOTES/INSIGHTS:

CHICKWEED

For you see your calling, brethren, that not many wise according to the flesh, not many mighty, not many noble, are called. But God has chosen the foolish things of the world to put to shame the wise, and God has chosen the weak things of the world to put to shame the things which are mighty; and the base things of the world and the things which are despised God has chosen, and the things which are not, to bring to nothing the things that are, that no flesh should glory in His presence.

1 Corinthians 1:26–29

There is a plant that grows all around my chicken coop called chickweed. The chickens love it. They will stick their beaks through the chicken wire to try to snatch a piece of it, and when I pluck it and throw it into the chicken run, they forget all about the scratch or feed that I put out for them, and they go for the chickweed. They gobble it down and eat every last leaf or stem.

The horses, however, have no taste for chickweed. They avoid it, graze around it, and even sometimes seemed annoyed by the chickweed in their pastures. They have no use for chickweed because they are not chickens. If they were chickens, they would see the value of chickweed for the tasty treat it is, and they would devour it just as quickly as the chickens do.

To the world, we Christians look like my chickens to the horses. We dig into the Word of God just as the chickens devour the chickweed. We love the Bible because it tells us about the love of our Savior, it feeds our souls and is sweet to our spirits. It is our necessary spiritual food. But to a world of horses, the Word of God is something to be avoided, and even be annoyed by. They don't want to take the time to learn of its value because they do not have the Spirit of God that gives understanding (1 Corinthians 1).

It is important that we try to persuade others of the importance of the Scriptures; it is God's love letter to all humanity. But whether they choose to dig in or not, we need to keep filling our souls and spirits with its truths and not worry if others think we are foolish. What God thinks is all that matters, and He has called us to be like chickens in a world full of horses. Enjoy your chickweed today.

THOUGHT-PROVOKER:

Are we digging into His Word and applying its principles to our lives? Are we more concerned about whether men think we are foolish, or that we are called by God and so live in and by His Word?

Dear Lord, thank You for Your Word and that we can dig into it and understand it because of the Holy Spirit indwelling us. Help us to not worry about looking foolish to the world, but to continue in it so that others see You get the glory for the lives You have made new. In Jesus' name, Amen.

NOTES/INSIGHTS:

CROSS POLLINATION

If anyone among you thinks he is religious, and does not bridle his tongue but deceives his own heart, this one's religion is useless. Pure and undefiled religion before God and the Father is this: to visit orphans and widows in their trouble, and to keep oneself unspotted from the world.

James 1:26–27

When we first moved to the farm, I decided to try my hand at gardening. Not just a few simple rows, but a big garden. Big enough that we put a fence around it to keep the deer and the rabbits out, and I had several rows of various kinds of vegetables. There were different kinds of squash, beans, tomatoes, cucumbers, and melons. I wanted to be able to have fresh vegetables all summer, and to put some back for the winter months too.

But I was a novice gardener, and I did not realize that my cucumbers were downwind from my watermelons. I did not realize that this was going to be an issue. When the first watermelons popped up, they had gorgeous, dark green rinds on the outside and I was so excited to watch them grow and mature. They grew big and round, and I could hardly wait to take the first ripe one inside and cut it open so we could enjoy that red, juicy melon. Imagine my disappointment when I cut into that very first watermelon, and it was completely white on the inside. No red juice dripping out as I cut through the rind, no red flesh inside. It was all completely white. The cucumbers had cross pollinated my watermelons and made them beautiful on the outside, but totally useless on the inside. Cross pollination caused my favorite summer melon to become colorless and tasteless.

When we cross pollinate the world's ideas with what God says, our religion—the outward expression of our inward beliefs—becomes useless as well. Our passage today tells us that we must bridle our tongues, visit orphans and widows, and keep ourselves unspotted from the world. Unspotted from the world—don't cross pollinate. It may make us look good on the outside, but we will be empty on the inside. We won't have the flavor or the life of a pure, meaningful relationship with God, and that means we will be useless when it comes to serving others in His kingdom.

Thought-provoker:

Where are we allowing the world to input its ideas into what we think we should be doing for God? Where is the cross pollination coming from, and how can we get back to a pure, unspotted relationship with Him?

Dear Lord, thank You for giving us Your Word to help us find the way to have a true relationship with You and how to keep ourselves unspotted from the world. Help us to not cross pollinate the world's ideas into our relationship with You, or how we interact with others. Your ways are best, help us to walk in them. In Jesus' name, Amen.

NOTES/INSIGHTS:

POISON OAK & CALAMINE

Remember the word to Your servant, upon which You have caused me to hope. This is my comfort in my affliction, for Your word has given me life.

Psalm 119: 49–50

One of the hazards of living on a farm with woods is poison oak. Because of an autoimmune disease, I am not able to take steroid shots for treatment, and antihistamines don't affect the rash. I try to be very careful to avoid poisonous plants, but sometimes, they are growing among the ground cover, and I come in contact with them while working on the farm.

The rash is quite uncomfortable. It itches, and it hurts. It keeps me from sleeping, and sometimes, if I am honest, it discourages me too. I can't do the things I normally do because the rash flares and causes even more discomfort when I get hot or sweat.

Thankfully, Calamine lotion helps. Calamine has a cooling property that calms the rash and irritation. There are days that I apply Calamine over and over, because the rash keeps irritating my skin and the Calamine is the only thing that soothes it. I apply it first thing in the morning, during the day, and even in the middle of the night when the itching wakes me.

There have been times in my life when sorrow has been like poison oak. I tried to avoid it, but it crept into the ground cover of my life, and it caused a full-blown reaction. It hurt, it irritated, and it disrupted my normal living. Nothing the world offered would help. Like the steroids and the antihistamines, the world's solutions to sorrow had no effect. I had to turn to the Calamine lotion of God's Word.

The Bible brought me comfort as I applied it to the wounds of sorrow in my soul. There were times I needed my heart to be soaked in the Word early in the morning, during the day, and even in the middle of the night, just to be able to keep going, to breathe the next breath and to take the next step. And the Word was always faithful to soothe my soul. No matter how many times I needed to apply it, it helped. It calmed the hurt and irritation, and even helped me to find rest.

Sorrow, much like a poison oak rash, does subside with time. Thankfully, seasons do pass, and pain doesn't keep its grip on us forever, whether it is a physical rash on the skin, or a piercing of the soul. And I am even more grateful that through those seasons, applying even more of the Word of God to our hearts soothes and comforts. May we find the comfort we need today as we turn to His Word.

Thought-provoker:

What Scriptures bring us comfort in times of sorrow? Do we need to apply more of it to help comfort our souls today?

Dear Lord, thank You for the Calamine of Your Word that soothes our souls when we are afflicted by sorrow. Help us to turn to it as often as we need to in the days ahead. In Jesus' name, Amen.

NOTES/INSIGHTS:

THE HURTING HORSE

*For God did not appoint us to wrath, but to obtain sal-
vation through our Lord Jesus Christ, who died for us, that
whether we wake or sleep, we should live together with Him.
Therefore comfort each other and edify one another, just as
you also are doing.*

1 Thessalonians 5:9–11

W e had two horses that were inseparable at our farm. One
was an older horse, and the other was a rescue. I don't admit to
understanding all about herd dynamics, but these two horses
definitely had a bond of companionship.

Sadly, the older horse's health deteriorated, and we had to
make the decision to have the veterinarian come for a final visit.
The rescued horse stayed right by her side, until the veterinarian
said it was time and the old horse needed to move to the field
where she would be buried. It was a slow walk to the field. As
we walked her out, we could hear the rescued horse whinnying
and pacing at the fence. As I watched, the other horses from
the herd surrounded him and gently moved him away from the
fence. They nickered to him, walked beside him, and led him
to a lush part of the pasture to eat with them. As he whinnied,

they would softly neigh back to him. They kept him in the middle of the herd all day and led him to the barn that night. In the morning, they were all standing around him, and they made sure he stayed with the herd for the next few days.

Those horses did what the church should do when one of our members sorrows. They surrounded and comforted him and let him know he was not alone. They didn't just keep him on the outskirts of the group but brought him in and loved on him in a horse sense. They provided protection, comfort, and companionship when he thought his world was coming apart. When he lost his companion, he gained a loving herd. They were gentle and patient with him as he grieved, and they continued to include him until he was able to regain his confidence. He still runs with that herd to this day.

Maybe today you are that rescued horse. Maybe you've lost a companion of a lifetime, or something has caused great sorrow in your life. I hope you will let the herd love on you, comfort you and encourage you as you hurt. Or maybe you are one of the herd. You see someone hurting, and they need you to accept them in, surround them with love and comfort and walk this journey with them as they grieve their loss. Be the herd someone needs today.

THOUGHT-PROVOKER:

Are we loving the hurting? Are we allowing others to comfort us when we are the hurting? Are we being the herd to those around us?

Lord, please help us to love those who hurt and be willing to be loved when we are hurting. Thank You for the comfort You provide through the church family You have given us. In Jesus' name, Amen.

FLASHLIGHT

For we walk by faith, not by sight.

2 Corinthians 5:7

When the days get shorter, I need a flashlight for the evening walk out to the barn to feed. It's not too terribly far, but it is a gravel path, and the ground is a little uneven. There are no lights between the house and the barn, so the flashlight helps me find my way without tripping or slipping in cold weather. The flashlight lights up the ground just ahead of me. It doesn't light up the entire path at one time, but just the path a few steps ahead of where I am. I depend on that light to avoid dips in the ground, black ice in winter, and puddles in the spring. It keeps me focused on the next step in front of me and makes the trip to the barn much easier by preventing me from getting hurt.

Faith is our spiritual flashlight. It doesn't light up miles and miles of the journey at one time, it illumines the next few steps. If we knew all that God has planned down the road, we might forge our own detours or be paralyzed by fear. Instead, God allows faith to enable us to take one step at a time, to stay focused where we are, and to trust Him to get us to the barn and back—to move us forward in ministry for His glory. We can't take credit for what the flashlight does, just as we can't take credit for the ways God leads us through life. He works through faith and trust as we take one step at a time.

Faith protects us too. When we walk in faith, we avoid the pitfalls of sin and regret. We don't get tripped up by circumstances. We won't fall into the puddles of despair or slip on the ice of discouragement when trials surround our path. We stay focused on the beam of faith, and we keep walking, one step at a time, trusting we will get where we need to go.

Another thing I love about my flashlight is that it is my daily companion in the dark. I pick it up and use it each night and it keeps lighting the way. Faith is a daily companion too. Each time we have faith, each time we trust God knows what He is doing in the midst of the darkness around us, faith keeps lighting the way.

Today, if you are struggling with doubt, wondering where God is or what He is doing, pick up your faith flashlight. Ask God to light the next step. He won't leave you in the dark.

Thought-provoker:

Are we picking up the flashlight of faith each day and allowing God to show us one step at a time?

Dear Lord, thank You that we walk by faith and not by sight. Thank You that You make a way when the world is dark, and we aren't sure where to go. Thank You that Your love won't leave us in the dark. Help us pick up the flashlight of faith today. In Jesus' name, Amen.

Notes/Insights:

Narrow Gate

Enter by the narrow gate; for wide is the gate and broad is the way that leads to destruction, and there are many who go in by it. Because narrow is the gate and difficult is the way which leads to life, and there are few who find it.

Matthew 7:13–14

We have a very small door on the chicken coop that only one chicken can go through at a time. We keep the door small so that, hopefully, we can keep large predators out and keep the chickens safe through the night. In the mornings when we open the door, all the chickens try to get through the door at once. But that is not how it works; each individual chicken has to make the choice for herself and go through the opening on her own. Then, each one comes out into the sunshine and enjoys the day.

We need to realize that there is a narrow gate that leads us to life as well. We cannot ask someone else to give us their faith. We each have to accept the Gospel on our own, just like the chickens have to choose to come through the small door and into the sunshine. Jesus tells us that He is the Way, the Truth and the Life and no one comes to the Father except by Him (John 14:6).

Some people think that it is awful that God makes only one Way, how unkind can He be that He won't accept anyone no matter how they try to get to heaven. But it is in His goodness and holiness that He only makes one Way. The price that He paid to make it possible for us to be restored through faith means that He gets to decide how that Way will be. His love for us paved the way to the narrow gate, and His sacrifice unlocks eternity when we are willing to surrender and walk through the narrow gate of His grace. Though the gate is narrow, it opens into a wide life in the joy and mercy of God. Just like my chickens can enjoy the sunshine, the grass, the feed, and water I provide for them, we also can enjoy the blessings of forgiveness, provision, and goodness that God has for us on the other side of the narrow gate of salvation.

The next time we hear the term *narrow-minded*, I hope it will remind us of the narrow gate that Christ opened for us to be able to spend eternity with Him in heaven and enjoy the blessings of a relationship with Him here on earth.

THOUGHT-PROVOKER:

Have we settled the matter of walking through the narrow gate of salvation through grace, or are we still bristling against His direction? If we have walked through the gate, are we sharing the Way with others so they can come through too?

Dear Lord, thank You for making salvation clear and narrow so we all can understand it by faith. Help us to share the Way with others today, and every day. In Jesus' name, Amen.

NOTES/INSIGHTS:

GOAT PEOPLE

All the nations will be gathered before Him, and He will separate them one from another, as a shepherd divides his sheep from the goats. And He will set the sheep on His right hand, but the goats on the left. Then the King will say to those on His right hand, "Come, you blessed of My Father, inherit the kingdom prepared for you from the foundation of the world."

Matthew 25:32–34

We have friends who love goats. Rob and Donna have a 130-acre farm where their goats have access to fresh water and all the grass they could desire. Rob and Donna look after their goats and make sure they are healthy and happy. Their goats know Rob's voice, and they will follow him in the pasture and go wherever he leads them. They trust Rob and Donna to take care of them and to provide for them. To be honest, I am not a real fan of goats. I have been chased by a Billy goat, I have seen goats fight with each other, and in some ways they intimidate me. I know that sounds funny coming from a horse person, but I understand how horses think—goats, not so much.

Scripture likens those who do not know Jesus as their Savior to goats. Those who have rebelled against God and His redemption, those who go their own ways and don't see the point of needing a Savior from their sin, these are likened to goats. Goats can be strong-willed, independent, and sometimes, aggressive. They challenge the norms of the herd, and they can be very stubborn. People who are lost without God can be these things too.

Instead of shunning goats, Rob and Donna love on them. They provide food, shelter, and water for them. The goats come to trust Rob and Donna, and by building those relationships, Rob and Donna get the goats to follow them to safety. And it's not just physical goats that Rob and Donna have a love for. They show genuine love to those around them who don't have a Savior. They build relationships with people who others may think are unlovely, difficult, or intimidating. Rob and Donna understand that the Great Commission includes telling every-one—even difficult goats. Especially difficult goats.

As I have spent more time with Rob and Donna at their farm, I have learned to accept goats. Rob and Donna are good teachers, and their methods work. Watching Rob and Donna love on people and bring them to Jesus is also a privilege. The world needs more goat lovers.

THOUGHT-PROVOKER:

Are we reaching the goats of this world with the love of Jesus or are we put off by their stubbornness or intimidated by their aggression? What do we need to do differently to boldly reach those who are challenging with the love of Jesus and the Gospel?

Lord, help us love the goats. They can be difficult and stubborn, but they need You and the redemption You provide through Your Son, Jesus Christ. Help us to build those relationships and give them the opportunity to know You. In Jesus' name, Amen.

NOTES/INSIGHTS:

Fly Mask

*I will set nothing wicked before my eyes; I hate the work
of those who fall away; It shall not cling to me. A perverse
heart shall depart from me; I will not know wickedness.*

Psalm 101:3–4

My horse gets annoyed by flies that land on his eyes. They
swarm around his eyes, pestering him, biting him, and making
him irritable and restless. These flies can cause infections, and
the irritation causes his eyes to water. In order to prevent the
infections and irritations, I put a fly mask on him. A fly mask is a
mesh cover that he can see through, but the flies cannot get past.
It is a simple piece of equipment that keeps the flies off his eyes
and keeps the infections away. I put it on his face each morning
before he leaves the barn, and he appreciates the relief it provides.

Scripture is like the fly mask. By putting it in front of our
eyes, by reading and learning it each day, it keeps our eyes protected from evil. When evil tries to invade our souls through
something we see, the filter of Scripture helps us to recognize it
for what it is and to step away from it. The wickedness cannot
infect us if we do not allow the flies of evil to land on our eyes
and cause irritation in our spirits.

Horses that have flies swarming their eyes are distracted and distressed. Sometimes, they will rub their faces on tree trunks, or roll in the dirt trying to get relief from the flies. Fly masks protect them from that distress, just as the Scriptures protect us from the irritations of temptations and sin in our lives. It also protects us from the wounds we inflict when we try to find relief on our own, just as the horses do with the tree trunks and dirt. When we are willing to put on the fly mask of the Scriptures, God protects us through the power of His Word, and He gives us the ability to escape those temptations (I Corinthians 10).

Before the flies of temptation and sin have the opportunity to infect us through our eyes today, we should put on the spiritual fly mask of God's Word. His Word is strong and more than capable of protecting us today if we make the decision to spend time in it and apply it.

Thought-provoker:

Are we applying the spiritual fly mask of Scripture to our eyes each day, or are we allowing the flies of evil to irritate and infect our lives?

Dear Lord, thank You for the protection Your Word provides to us each day as we read it and apply it. Just as the horses need the fly masks, we need Your Word to protect us. Help us to put it on each day. In Jesus' name, Amen.

NOTES/INSIGHTS:

FEAR OF THE KNIGHT

*Oh, clap your hands, all you peoples! Shout to God with
the voice of triumph! For the Lord Most High is awesome;
He is a great King over all the earth.*

Psalm 47:1–2

She stands almost 17 hands tall, solid black, with a wide
heart girth and a strong back. She is one of the fastest rackers
I have ever seen, and she moves with intimidating force. If she
is coming at you, you get out of the way. Fear of the Knight,
her registered name, makes her seem invincible, unapproachable. She stands tall and powerful. The issue with Java is that
while she is strong, she loves people. Once you get to know
her, you realize her barn name, Java, is much more fitting. She
is like sitting down to a cup of coffee with a friend. Yes, she is
big, but she is a gentle giant. If you are having a conversation
around the barn, she sticks her head into the group as if she is
listening to every word. She loves scratches from strangers, and
if you are a kid with an apple, you've just made a friend for life.

Just seeing her name on paper, or seeing her racking impres-
sively around the arena, Java seems intimidating. If you only
know her by her name, you get the wrong impression. If you

just watch her from a distance, you think she is strong and aloof. Just like some people do with God.

God has many names—majestic names like Elohim (Supreme One), Jehovah (I AM), El Shaddai (God Almighty). And He is all those things. People get the impression that He is invincible, unapproachable, intimidating. Some believe that He is far away and too powerful to be, well, personal. But, just like Java, He is also Abba (Daddy), Friend and Counselor. You can sit down to a cup of coffee and pour your heart out to Him, and He hears every word. He not only listens, but He cares. When we get to know God on a personal level, by spending time with Him, we correct our perception. God is not some big, frowny-faced, intimidating being in the heavens—He is personal, up close, and loving. If we have the wrong idea of Him, it's because we do not know Him like we should.

Yes, He is a mighty King, a powerful Sovereign, a strong and awesome God. He is also our Savior and friend. Spend some time with God, your personal loves-you-beyond-imagination God, who wants us to see He is awesome, and that is something for us to be excited about, not afraid. Clap your hands and enjoy the victory He gives you today.

THOUGHT-PROVOKER:

Do we perceive God as intimidating and unapproachable, or do we know Him personally? What perceptions of Him need to change in our hearts today?

Dear Lord, thank You that You are awesome, powerful, and mighty, but You are also our Savior and Friend. Help us to always be in awe of You, but not afraid. Help us to know You better today. In Jesus' name, Amen.

NOTES/INSIGHTS:

THE LONG TRAIL RIDE

A man's heart plans his way, but the Lord directs his steps.
Proverbs 16:9

It was supposed to be a two-hour trail ride. We had done this trail before, and we tacked up and headed out with no problems. We were enjoying the nature all around us, the beautiful canopy and shade provided by the trees, the interesting rocks, and crevices in the woods as we went. But somehow, we missed the turnaround. We got to two hours and realized we were nowhere near the stables and parking lot where we had started. We eventually came to the end of the trail; a black asphalt road was in front of us, and we weren't sure where it went or how busy it would be. We had no choice but to turn around and go back.

What was supposed to be a two-hour ride turned into almost five. We were getting tired, and the sun kept getting lower. We joked about needing to remember a spotlight for the trail pack next time, and I quietly thought it might be worth putting a tracking beacon in the trailer so I could find it from anywhere.

Finally, we broke into a field and saw some of the most gorgeous landscape and sunset Tennessee has to offer. The colors were amazing. That trip has become one of our favorite memories from that summer, all because we wound up having to take a U-turn.

Sometimes it seems we are going backwards. We were making progress and suddenly we realize we have missed the mark. We come to the end of the trail we had planned, and we must turn around. But God is not surprised by U-turns. He knows exactly where we are, where we need to be and how we are going to get there. In those moments, look for the landscape and the sunset. God may have had you turn around so you can take in a wonderful moment, a fantastic memory that otherwise, you would have missed. Those U-turns are so much better than ending up on an asphalt road in the middle of nowhere.

Today, as we evaluate where we are, where we think we are going, take a moment and pause. Whisper a prayer, ask God to lead you, even if you think it is back the way you came. Sometimes, we need to get back to the fundamentals of our faith, stop being so focused on moving, and take some time to see which way He wants us to go, and you won't need a beacon to get there.

THOUGHT-PROVOKER:

Does it seem like we are on a long ride to nowhere spiritually? Take some time and evaluate where you are, where you want to go, and what God is asking you to do.

Dear Lord, thank You that You see the whole trail, not just the part we are on. When U-turns happen, help us to look for the sunset—that moment we would have missed if we had gone our own way. In Jesus' name, Amen.

NOTES/INSIGHTS:

DONKEY EARS

But be doers of the word, and not hearers only, deceiving yourselves.

James 1:22

Our miniature donkey has the cutest ears, but they are huge! Her ears are the same size as the length of her face, and most of the time she keeps them upright. She hears everything, from the kitten meowing at the other end of the barn, to the horses neighing in the neighboring pasture. She hears my footsteps as I approach the barn each morning, and she greets me with a hungry, *Hee-haw!* She is a good girl, a sweet personality—unless you put the halter on her.

Sunshine knows the halter means she is going to work. She hears me as I coax her out of her stall and down the hallway of the barn to the door that leads outside. She hears me talking to her, whistling to her and, sometimes, getting stern with her. She hears every word. The problem is she does not want to leave the barn to go to work. She hears everything I tell her about how it is sunny outside, she is going to enjoy being outside with the other horses, and all the good things that will come from going outside and working. She just doesn't want to do it. She digs her heels in, sets her weight back on her hind legs and lifts her head in the air. Even as a miniature donkey, she is very strong when she is being stubborn, and it takes a lot of energy to get her moving again. Sometimes, I sit and stare at her as she pulls back on the halter, and I just have to wait it out. She is not budging, and there is no sense in wasting the energy it takes to make her take a step.

I wonder if we are a lot more like Sunshine, the donkey, than we care to admit. God's Word tells us the things we are supposed to do—love one another, pray for each other, help those in need, and so many more things that make up the Christian walk—and we hear every word. We just don't want to do it. Just like Sunshine, we dig in our heels and sit on our haunches. Maybe we even bray and complain about the things God asks us to do being so hard, when in reality, they are for our good.

Today, instead of using our donkey haunches, let's use our donkey ears to hear it all, and then respond with energy and enthusiasm to do the work, instead of fighting it. Let's be like Sunshine in a good way, having our ears up and hearing, and doing things to bring about His kingdom.

THOUGHT-PROVOKER:

Which way are we like Sunshine, the donkey? Are we digging our heels in and resisting what God is asking of us today, or are we hearing it and responding with enthusiasm and energy?

Dear Lord, help us not to just hear, but be willing and then doing, all that You have for us today. In Jesus' name, Amen.

Notes/Insights:

HOT WALKER

Therefore, by the deeds of the law no flesh will be justified
in His sight, for by the law is the knowledge of sin.

Romans 3:20

There is a device that is used to exercise horses called a Hot Walker. It is a circular walker to which two to six horses can be tied, depending on its size, and each horse space has a hot wire that drags behind the horses' hind feet. If they stop, refuse to walk, or do not keep pace with the walker, the wire hits their hind legs and gives them a small electrical charge to motivate them to keep going. I am personally not a fan of the Hot Walker, but for some, it is a necessity because of the number of horses they need to exercise, or limited space available to exercise them.

There is another type of Walker that isn't hot. The horses are tied to it, but they power the mechanism to turn it, and there is no wire dragging behind their feet. The horses have to work together to turn the Walker, and I have seen some trainers partner up experienced horses with new ones to teach the new ones to walk willingly with the Walker and get their exercise without being jolted to keep going.

Seeing the different Walkers reminds us of two ways to relate to God. In one way, we walk in legalism. The rules and traditions of men drag behind us and nip at our heels if we stop to question, need to slow down for a time, or if we rebel against traditions to find a deeper relationship. The Hot Walker relation to God makes us feel that we are only worthy if we keep up with all the dos and don'ts, the list that determines whether we are making it or not.

The other Walker reminds us that we can walk in grace. We can walk at a comfortable speed, and we have the benefit of others who have more experience and wisdom to walk with us and help us learn the way. When we stumble, stop to question, or maybe even rebel a bit, grace is extended. Those walking with us pause to help us regain our composure; they encourage us to start walking again, and there is no zap of punishment for not measuring up in that moment.

We need grace. We need to extend it to those who are walking this journey with us, and we need them to extend it to us too. May we find ourselves willingly walking in relationship with our Heavenly Father and not depending on the rules to determine our worth.

THOUGHT-PROVOKER:

Which spiritual Walker are you working today? Are you working from a place of lists or grace?

Dear Lord, please help us to willingly enter into growth and maturity with You and not depend on lists of rules and traditions to keep us in line. Help us to trust You and to accept the help of others You place on this journey with us to help us become strong. In Jesus' name, Amen.

125

NOTES/INSIGHTS:

FROSTED SHADOWS

This is the message which we have heard from Him and declare to you, that God is light and in Him is no darkness at all. If we say that we have fellowship with Him, and walk in darkness, we lie and do not practice the truth. But if we walk in the light as He is in the light, we have fellowship with one another, and the blood of Jesus Christ His Son cleanses us from all sin.

1 John 1:5–7

There is a spot near the barn that does not get much sunlight until the very late afternoon. Because of this, a shadow is cast across the ground for much of the morning, and when it is cold, the frost is able to stay on the grass much longer in this area than anywhere else around the barn.

On those strange spring mornings when it starts out cold, but then turns nice and sunny by mid-morning, the frost *survives* by staying in the shadows. Anywhere there is sunlight, the frost disappears. The grass around the barn pops up green and lively, but the grass in the shadow is still thick with frost and ice. It looks dead and bitter as it shrivels in the cold.

The green grass is much more attractive than the grass that

is covered with the hoary frost. The warmth of the sun is much more appealing than the cold lifelessness of the shadow. The smell and feel of spring warm our senses and awaken hope with the expectation of warmer days, flowers, and light spring rains. When I find myself in the shadow spot by the barn, I want to move out where it is warmer, brighter, and more inviting.

"God is light and in Him is no darkness at all." There are no shadows in God's presence; no place where our hearts can stay cold, bitter, and lifeless. We find fellowship when we move out of the shadows. When we choose to step into the light of His presence, our hearts are warmed with forgiveness and grace, and we cannot stay hard and cold. His light helps us to grow and thrive, to be fruitful and lively. And His light gives us hope. We look forward to the warmth of our relationship with Him, and we find ourselves moving away from the cold darkness of the shadows.

As we walk through our day, we should step out of the shadows of hopelessness, ungratefulness, and discouragement and step into the light. After all, that is where our Heavenly Father is, and He will warm us with His love and give us hope.

Thought-provoker:

Why are we staying in the shadows where our hearts are getting cold and bitter? Where can we decide to step into the light of God's presence and have Him change our attitude or heart today?

Dear Lord, thank You that You are light and that there is no darkness—no bitterness, no discouragement—in Your presence. Help us choose to step into the light of Your presence today. In Jesus' name, Amen.

Notes/Insights:

SHEDDING

To everything there is a season, a time for every purpose under heaven.

Ecclesiastes 3:1

In February it's wintertime, and it is still cold. Sometimes it is very cold. And yet, my friend Renee pointed out the other day that the horses are already starting to shed out their winter coats. You would think that they would need those extra hairs—especially when it is twenty degrees at night. But every time we groom the horses, they are shedding.

It really makes no sense, and yet God designed those winter coats to do exactly what they are doing. The horses are keeping their undercoat—the fur underneath that keeps them warm and dry, but they are losing the outer hair. Their bodies are being prepared for the next season—spring. God won't allow them to lose the undercoat until the days lengthen and the temperatures warm up, but He is allowing them to shed the hair that would mat them up, that would tangle and knot, and He is letting them shed it off before it becomes a serious problem.

He does the same for us, dear believers. We think it is a time of dark, cold winter in our lives, and we need every layer of protection we can get. But God in His wisdom, knows that another season is just around the corner, and those things that we are so desperately holding onto to protect us will just become mats and knots in our lives in the next season. So, He allows them to shed. He allows them to be brushed away from our lives, and we need to trust His judgment. He won't take away what we need, but maybe what we need is less of something that is complicating our lives, and we just can't see it because of the season we are in. There is hope knowing the next season is just around the corner, and there is peace in knowing that He will not take something away without preparing us for something better.

Let the shedding begin. Trust the Lord as He brushes away those things that we don't need to hold onto anymore and know that He is preparing us for a new season of joy and peace, Hang in there, friends, spring is coming.

Thought-provoker:

What things do we need to trust God to shed from our lives, even if it doesn't make sense in the moment? What new season do we have to look forward to?

Dear Lord, thank You for not allowing the knots and mats that come from holding onto our protective layers. Help us to trust You for what we need, and to trust You to take what we don't. There is a new season right around the corner, and You have Your hand all over it. Help us to look forward, even if it is hard to understand what You are doing in the moment. We love You. In Jesus' name, Amen.

NOTES/INSIGHTS:

LONE STAR

Therefore, you also be ready, for the Son of Man is coming at an hour you do not expect. Who then is a faithful and wise servant, whom his master made ruler over his household, to give them food in due season? Blessed is that servant whom his master, when he comes, will find so doing.

Matthew 24:44–46

Lone Star is a beautiful bay horse that has deep eyes and a gorgeously long tail. His forelock poofs up above his eyelids, and even though he has some age on him, you can still see his shoulders muscles ripple as he canters in for his dinner in the evening. He is a retired hunter-jumper horse that belongs to a friend of ours. He has seen all there is to see on the competition circuit, and he is now retired and enjoying the pasture life. He likes being retired, grazing on grass, and munching on hay when it gets dropped for him and his pasture-mates in the morning and evenings. He drinks deeply from the water trough, and he sticks his tongue out at anyone who watches him take a drink. He is a good horse, with good manners and a funny disposition that makes almost everyone like him.

When Lone Star was younger, his owner was able to come

see him more often and work with him regularly. Lone Star was always happy to see her, and he enjoyed the forelock rubs and the Nutter Butters (his favorite treat). But because of a job change and building a house, she had to move farther away and now she doesn't get to come see him quite as often.

That doesn't change Lone Star. Even though she is not around, he still remembers the ground manners she taught him, and he behaves himself around the other horses. He keeps an eye on the front gate to see if she will come, and he still gets excited when he sees her car pull up the drive.

Believers need to be like Lone Star. Even when we have grown in our faith and have some age on us, we should still be expecting the Lord's return. We should still be living the way He taught us to, standing strong in His love and leaning on the grace and mercy He has poured into us.

Lone Star doesn't forget who he belongs to, and he still gets excited to see her. We should remember Whose we are and be excited that He is coming back for us. And we should still be glancing at the sky, waiting, hoping to catch a glimpse of Him who loves us.

THOUGHT-PROVOKER:

Are we waiting expectantly for Jesus to come back, or have we given up and decided to do our own thing?

Dear Lord, thank You for the promise that You are coming back for us. Help us to remember to live the way You taught us to, to behave among others as You have asked, and to keep an eye on the sky to see Your return. Thank You for the hope we have in You today and always. In Jesus' name, Amen.

NOTES/INSIGHTS:

THE FIRE PIT

Flee sexual immorality. Every sin that a man does is out-side the body, but he who commits sexual immorality sins against his own body. Or do you not know that your body is the temple of the Holy Spirit who is in you, whom you have from God, and you are not your own?

1 Corinthians 6:18–19

Because we also have woods on our property, we have to trim branches and bushes and those trimmings are added to the brush pile. Early spring and late fall, the two times we usually do the pruning and trimming, we obtain a burn permit, and we drag the branches and such to the burn pit on our farm. Our burn pit is a dugout lined with brick and rock so that the fire stays in the pit. It is a well-built boundary for the fire, and it keeps the fire from spreading where it should not be. We invite some friends over, and we enjoy an evening, celebrating that the trimming is done and enjoying fellowship together. We are careful to heed burn bans and wind warnings, as we do not want the fire spreading and causing damage.

A few years ago, a farm not too far from us had a tragic result from their fire. They did not heed the fire ban from our local fire departments, and they did not burn within a fire pit, and the out-of-control fire burned half of their hay field before the firefighters could get it out. They lost the revenue from the crops that were burned, and their barn was also damaged by the fire.

God has placed a firm boundary around the fire of physical passion. He says that fire needs to burn within a marriage—a place where it is contained and enjoyed (Hebrews 13:4). But, when men and women do not heed the boundaries and bans God has put on sexual desire, tragic damage happens. Reputations are burned, trust is destroyed, relationships go up in smoke and what should be something sacred and celebrated becomes a disaster. God knows that physical passion needs to be fostered within the boundaries of commitment and security that only come within a marriage.

When anyone decides to burn those desires outside of that boundary, tragedy happens. God has given the permit of marriage to allow those desires to burn brightly and beautifully, and to be celebrated within a union that keeps romance and love alive. Anywhere else, with anyone else, only causes heartbreak and leaves a trail of broken bodies and spirits. Living within the protected, permitted, well-built boundaries of marriage, the fires of passion will serve us well. Anything else is a disaster in the making.

THOUGHT-PROVOKER:

Are we keeping the fire of physical desire in the boundaries of marriage, whether that means only in our marriage, or waiting until we are married? What protections do we need to raise to keep our marriage fires holy?

Dear Lord, thank You for the boundaries You have given to protect us and to give us the beauty of physical passion within a marriage. Help us keep those boundaries in place and honor You. In Jesus' name, Amen.

NOTES/INSIGHTS:

THE STORM

But as they sailed, He fell asleep. And a windstorm came down on the lake, and they were filling with water, and were in jeopardy. And they came to Him and awoke Him, saying, "Master, Master, we are perishing!" Then He arose and rebuked the wind and the raging of the water. And they ceased, and there was a calm. But He said to them, "Where is your faith?" And they were afraid, and marveled, saying to one another, "Who can this be? For He commands even the winds and water, and they obey Him!"

Luke 8:23–25

As I am sitting here typing, sixty-mile per hour winds are gusting past our house, around the barn and down the hill in the back pasture. The storm has already dropped enough rain to form a pond in the front pasture, send the creek over its banks in the back, knock down two trees, and break the fence. The horses are fine—they are in the barn—and the chickens ran for cover in the coop. But it sure does feel like the wind is going to blow everything off its foundations.

Thankfully, the foundations of the house and the barn run deep, and they are still standing, even after heavy winds and rain.

Even when we feel like we are in jeopardy, He rises and rebukes the wind and the raging water, and everything must be at peace. I know that the winds will stop, and the sun will shine tomorrow. But my faith is tested during the storm. Where is He? He is present, I know this in my head, but my heart challenges while the winds blow. When hard news comes from an unexpected place, when the doctor calls and it's not what we wanted to hear, He asks me, "Where is your faith?" The foundation of my relationship with Him—a gift He gave me when I surrendered to Him as Lord—where does it go during the storm? It runs deep, and I must trust that even when trees fall and fences break, He is still here. Even when syndromes are attached to ones that we love, or sickness becomes a real-time issue, He is still in the boat. When we are concerned about a lawsuit, or any other number of trials threaten to sink my ship, He is bigger, stronger, and more powerful than anyone can imagine.

So, in the midst of the storm, I can sit calmly and tell another account of His faithfulness. Even when life throws unexpected, unwanted storms—I can wait in the boat, knowing He will get me to the other side. He is bigger than the storm. And the foundations of faith run deep because of the Savior Who loves me.

THOUGHT-PROVOKER:

Are we trusting Him or fretting about the storm? Where is our faith today?

Lord, thank You that You are always bigger, stronger, and more powerful than any of our storms. Help our faith to run deep, even when it's dark and we are afraid. Help us to always know nothing can separate us from You and Your love. In Jesus' name, Amen.

Notes/Insights:

THE CLEAN UP

Let nothing be done through selfish ambition or conceit,
but in lowliness of mind let each esteem others better than
himself. Let each of you look out not only for his own interests,
but also for the interests of others.

Philippians 2:3–4

The day after the really bad storm came through, there was quite a bit of clean up that needed to be done at the farm. The corner of the barn roof was peeled back, we had a fence that was completely down, there were pieces of walls and a roof from a mangled shed sticking up out of ground, and there were several trees down. Normally, I am a do-it-yourself kind of gal, but looking around the farm after the storm, I knew we were going to need help. I put out a text message to friends and family, hoping for a few people to come and give us a hand moving the things that were too big for one person and a tractor. The phone started ringing, and before I knew it, fourteen volunteers had shown up to help. They brought chain saws for the trees, gloves and shovels to help with the fence, and power tools to help with disassembling the shed and putting the barn roof back together. I watched as they paired off and each took a project. They came to check on us and they gave of themselves to help put our farm back together.

There was nothing for them to gain—they came because they cared. No one was bragging about how much they could help, they just got to work, and restored the soul of a storm-weary farm girl—me—in our community. Hammers, drills, shovels and tractor noises were a testament to all the work that was done. They came and looked out for our interests, knowing that we couldn't do all this alone.

The church community is like our farm friends. There should be no braggarts boasting about how much they do. We don't show up for each other during trials and sorrow to try to gain anything. We show up for each other because we care, and because Jesus encourages us to look after each other while we wait for Him to return (1 Thessalonians 5). Sometimes, we show up and we sit with them in a hospital waiting room. We pray as tears stream down our faces, hurting with each other because of loss. Sometimes, we have to get to work, repairing storm damage, dropping off groceries, making a meal, mowing a lawn, or taking any number of other opportunities God gives us to check in on each other and selflessly be the hands and feet of Christ. We become the cleanup crews that encourage and esteem others, and in doing these things, we put His love into action.

THOUGHT-PROVOKER:

What are ways that we can selflessly help others around us?

Lord, thank You for allowing us to show up for each other, to look after each other when difficult times come. Thank You for the opportunity to show You to those around us and make a difference as Your church. In Jesus' name, Amen.

NOTES/INSIGHTS:

SUNSHINE, PART TWO

Therefore take up the whole armor of God, that you may be able to withstand in the evil day, and having done all, to stand. Stand therefore, having girded your waist with truth, having put on the breastplate of righteousness, and having shod your feet with the preparation of the gospel of peace; above all, taking the shield of faith with which you will be able to quench all the fiery darts of the wicked one. And take the helmet of salvation, and the sword of the Spirit, which is the word of God.

Ephesians 6:13–17

You've already been introduced to Sunshine, the miniature donkey with a big personality that lives on our farm. Sunshine has a very interesting habit. Each morning after I let her out of her stall, she finds the driest section of dirt in the paddock, buckles her knees, and drops down into the dirt. She rolls from side to side, grunting and wagging her tail as she covers herself completely in dust. She makes sure every bit of her coat is covered in dust. She then gets up, shakes, and trots off happily to the pasture to begin her day of grazing and gallivanting out with the horses.

Sunshine covers herself with dust because she knows that

protects her from the gnats. The thicker her fur is with dirt, the less likely the gnats will be able to get to her to skin to bite her. She also knows if she misses a spot, the gnats are likely to congregate there and bite her, so she makes sure she is completely covered.

The armor of God protects us completely, but we need to make sure that we take all of it. Truth, righteousness, preparation of the gospel, faith, the knowledge of salvation and the Word of God are all components of our armor. If one is missing, we become vulnerable. We must not allow lies to cloud our judgment, or we can become disillusioned in our faith. We need Christ's righteousness, as well as the power of the Gospel, to protect our hearts from discouragement and ungratefulness. We need faith and the knowledge of salvation to protect our minds from distraction, insecurity, and deceit. We need the Word of God to define us, to defend us, and to strengthen us to stand against the onslaught that comes during these evil days.

Just like Sunshine does every morning, let us take a few moments with our Almighty Captain, the Lord of all eternity, and make sure we are covered. From the top of our heads to our toes, let us be covered in the armor that He provides so that we can stand with Him as He secures our victory.

Thought-provoker:

Are we taking the time to be sure we are covered in the Armor of God each day, or are we leaving ourselves vulnerable to the bites and wounds of the enemy?

Dear Lord, thank You for Your armor that protects us. Please help us to take time each day to put it on by spending time with You so that we are ready to stand. In Jesus' name, Amen.

NOTES/INSIGHTS:

REINS

A time to weep, and a time to laugh; a time to mourn, and a time to dance.

Ecclesiastes 3:4

I had an interesting trail ride the other day. Everything was going along normally. I was sitting relaxed in the saddle and enjoying the peace and quiet. When I gave a gentle tap on the rein, it fell loose in my hand. The rein had come loose of the bridle, and when I tugged on it, it gave way and came off. Trying to steer a horse with one rein is very interesting. Fortunately, my mount is also leg-trained, so I was able to pull off to the side of the trail, get him to stop, and then I dismounted and fixed the rein. I have seen others not have such a fortunate outcome. A friend of mine was riding her horse in the barrel pattern when the rein came off, and her horse took off for the back of the arena. She pulled the one rein she had, which sent her horse into a tailspin, and they rapidly circled through the arena to the fence. Her horse had enough sense to stop, but not before scaring the spectators and causing her to yell wildly and pull frantically to avoid the accident about to happen.

It takes two reins to steer a horse straight. It takes both sorrow and joy to keep us grounded. If all we ever had was sorrow, we would become discouraged with life. When the Israelites were wandering in the wilderness because of their rebellious hearts, Scripture tells us, *"...the soul of the people became very discouraged on the way. And the people spoke against God and against Moses...."* (Numbers 21:4–5). But if all we had was joy, then we would take our blessings for granted, and we would not acknowledge God as we should. The writer of Proverbs says, *Two things I request of You (deprive me not before I die): Remove falsehood and lies far from me; give me neither poverty nor riches—feed me with the food allotted to me; Lest I be full and deny You, and say, "Who is the Lord?" or lest I be poor and steal, and profane the name of my God.* Proverbs 30:7-9

It takes both joy and sorrow for our lives to move forward. We learn from them both that God is God, God is good, and God is big. We learn of His love in the good times, and the hard ones. As we walk between the reins of sorrow and joy, we learn to appreciate the trail and the One who is with us every step of the way, no matter what those steps may be.

THOUGHT-PROVOKER:

Are we thankful for the sorrows as well as the joys? Where do we see the hand of God working through both?

Dear Father, thank You for the wisdom of being guided by both the sorrows and joys of life so that we keep our eyes on You and appreciate the blessings, as well as the depths. Help us to trust You as we move forward today. In Jesus' name, Amen.

NOTES/INSIGHTS:

THE JACKHAMMER

Create in me a clean heart, O God, and renew a steadfast spirit within me.

Psalm 51:10

Because of where we live, there is a lot of rock. We have surface rocks that poke through the ground in our backyard, and we have deep rock that keeps grass roots shallow in certain parts of the pastures and hayfield. These rocks can cause issues, from minor inconveniences to dangerous situations. Some of them stick up just far enough that they can cause a person or an animal to stumble, because they are high enough to trip over, but low enough that they are hidden in the grass. Some others jut straight up out of the ground and are a hazard for the mower and Bush Hogs. They can damage blades, or parts of the rocks can come loose and be projectiles thrown from under the mower. So, when my husband's friend offered us a jackhammer to borrow for the week, we took him up on it.

Every day after work, my husband went out and worked the jackhammer. The jackhammer was too big for me to handle alone, but my husband did just fine. He worked away, breaking up the rock that stuck out of the ground, and then he would go deeper to break up the deep rock that would eventually work its way to the surface. There were piles of rock in the backyard, in the barnyard, and near the driveway. After he had pulverized the rock, he would pick up all the pieces and haul them away in the tractor bucket.

Once the rock was removed from the yard, my husband filled in the holes with good dirt. Some grass seed sprinkled on the spots and some time, and no one will ever know there had been a rock there that was capable of disabling farm equipment. The mower will go over good hay grass with ease this summer, and the yard will be so much prettier, a field of grass without rocks jutting through and breaking up the lush green grass.

In Scripture, God tells the Israelites that He will take their heart of stone and replace it with a heart of flesh (Ezekiel 36:26). God is the only one big enough to jackhammer away the stubbornness that creeps into our hearts and makes us hard to His will. We can't will it away or try to handle it ourselves. We must yield to the One who is strong enough to take it away and give us something better. Peace, surrender, and healing come from yielding our rocky hearts to Him. I hope my heart will be just as beautiful as our rock-less yard in the eyes of my loving Father. I hope yours will too.

THOUGHT-PROVOKER:

Are we giving our stubbornness over to Him to change and heal, or are we tenaciously holding onto our rocky hearts? Where does He need to work in us today?

Dear Lord, thank You that You can change our rocky hearts into beautiful fields of love and mercy. Help us to allow You to do Your work in us today. In Jesus' name Amen.

NOTES/INSIGHTS:

BUDDY

Let your conduct be without covetousness; be content with such things as you have. For He Himself has said, "I will never leave you nor forsake you."

Hebrews 13:5

Buddy is a Haflinger with a broad chest, long flowing mane, and a pony whinny. He likes everyone, but he had a little secret when he came to the farm. Buddy likes the grass on the other side of the fence better than the grass inside it. Because of his broad chest and stocky build, Buddy learned he could push on the fence and lean it over enough to reach the grass on the other side. The fence doesn't bounce back after it gets pushed on, and it got to the point that the other horses were able to jump over the lowered fence and could have gotten themselves into danger. Since we want all the horses to be safe, we had to address Buddy's issue.

We replaced the posts and then added electric tape around the top of the fence. Buddy watched us as we worked to make the fence a true boundary to keep him and his pasture-mates safe. And there was nothing wrong with the grass in the pasture. We were not depriving the horses of anything they needed, but Buddy was discontent with what he had.

The day we finished installing the fence, my husband and I went out to the pasture to check on the horses. As soon as Buddy saw us, he headed straight for the fence where he had pushed it down before. He leaned his broad chest into the fence and began to push with his strong hind legs. And then it happened. He touched the electric tape and got zapped. The surprise of the shock sent him reeling backwards, his back feet tangled, and he wound up on his back with all four feet in the air. My husband chuckled at him and said that he hoped Buddy learned his lesson as he flipped himself upright and took off for the far side of the pasture.

Buddy hasn't touched the fence since. He has learned to be content with what he has because he doesn't like the shock that comes from reaching for what he shouldn't. Sometimes I wish there were a visible fence to help us with our discontent. The times when we keep reaching for something outside what God has provided for us, something that we don't really need, but we just have to have. More than once discontent has left us sitting on our backsides, wondering why we were willing to pay such a high price for something that leaves us dissatisfied in the end. I hope that we will be like Buddy and learn to be content with what we have so we can avoid getting zapped because of our discontent.

THOUGHT-PROVOKER:

Where are we pushing the boundaries because of discontent? Where do we need to change our desires to live within the blessings God has already given us?

Dear Lord, please help us to be content with the blessings You have given us and to not try to push for something that we truly don't need. In Jesus' name, Amen.

Notes/Insights:

THE WINTER WATER BUCKETS

Bear one another's burdens, and so fulfill the law of Christ.
Galatians 6:2

Winter can be a trying time. Not only do I need to contend with extra layers of clothing to keep me warm and the animals needing extra hay while they are turned out, I also have to work extra at keeping water available for all the animals. The main water lines in the barn are not insulated enough to keep them from freezing, so I need to drain the water lines in the barn before it gets below freezing to prevent burst pipes. The man who designed our barn knew about the winter weather here, and the pipes, so he put an extra faucet in a heated area. When it is very cold outside, we still have water access in the barn, but only at that faucet. I am very grateful the former owner designed for that. I am also grateful that my husband helps carry the five-gallon buckets full of water to the water troughs. I am a little on the short side, and hoisting and carrying those buckets can be exhausting for me. Ten trips to each trough to fill them, and more than one trough needs water, and well, you get the idea.

My husband, however, is a six-foot two triathlete. He trains year-round and his legs are long enough that he doesn't have to hoist a bucket high to keep from tripping over it. He carries two buckets at a time without getting tired. He can fill a trough in no time and still be smiling. I tend to be grunting due to the effort.

His help makes wintertime bearable. His kindness toward me as he strides back and forth with those buckets is a bonus that makes me love him even more. As Christians, we should be kindly helping each other carry those burden buckets. If someone is hurting, we should be carrying the bucket of grief, walking alongside them, and letting them know they are not alone. If someone is sick, has had surgery, or is going through something that seems like a bleak winter, we can bring meals, have prayer with them, and be encouraging. Doing these things makes the winter seasons of suffering more bearable. Doing these things bonds His church together and shows the world the love they are missing.

As we go through different seasons together, I hope we will be mindful of those who are in the winter seasons of life, even if the earthly sun is shining and the sky is blue. Let us be aware of the burdens that some are carrying, and let us pick up those buckets and give them a hand. Let's be bucket carriers.

THOUGHT-PROVOKER:

Who needs us to help them carry deep burdens today? How can we come alongside and kindly help?

Dear Lord, thank You that You didn't leave us to walk this life in solitary, but You gave us the privilege of being bucket carriers. Help us to carry and help us to let others carry buckets for us in our times of winter. In Jesus' name, Amen.

Notes/Insights:

THE BARN CATS

"Again, I say to you that if two of you agree on earth con-
cerning anything that they ask, it will be done for them by
My Father in heaven. For where two or three are gathered
together in My name, I am there in the midst of them."
Matthew 18:19–20

We have three barn cats. Teddy is the oldest, a big Tabby cat
with a sweet heart and a laid-back disposition. We have referred
to Teddy many times as a lover not a fighter. Our daughter
found him when he was a kitten, and the owner gifted him to
our daughter as a Christmas present. Teddy loves to be with
people and would rather get treats than catch rats, although he
is quite an avid hunter when he needs to be. Ricky is the second
cat, a husky Maine Coon-looking boy who is very athletic and
quick. He is quite serious about most things but loves to be
petted. We have joked that Ricky is the best farm dog we've
ever had. He comes when he is called, he sits on command,
and he even helps to round up a wayward horse by running
around its feet without getting kicked. Dolly is our newest cat.
She was a gift from a friend, and while I thought I didn't need
another cat; this spunky calico has won over my heart and

has proven to be a good mouser in the barn. She still has that kittenish pounce, and her developing coordination and antics have led to many moments of joy and laughter.

All three of them are very different in personality and demeanor, but the three of them all agree on one thing—the top of the stacked hay is the best place for an afternoon nap. All three will climb up there and lay in a circle with their faces toward the middle. While they may pounce on each other and swat playfully at each other's faces out and about in the barnyard, when they get up on the hay, they are all agreed that peace and unity make for a good afternoon passing.

There are many different types of personalities in the church— God made each of us unique and special. We may be laid-back, serious, or spunky, but when we come together to pray and we are united in our spirits, asking for things that only God can do, He is there in the midst. Just as our barn cats come together for afternoon rest, we can come together to ask the God of the universe to do the impossible and watch Him work through the power of prayer.

THOUGHT-PROVOKER:

Are we taking the time to be together and pray? When we are together, what are we praying for God to do?

Dear Lord, thank You that even as different as we may be, when we come together to pray, You are in the midst of us. Help us to take the time to be together, to pray together, and to watch You do the impossible. In Jesus' name, Amen.

NOTES/INSIGHTS:

THE MUD PUDDLE

*Jesus answered and said to her, "If you knew the gift of God,
and who it is who says to you, 'Give Me a drink,' you would
have asked Him, and He would have given you living water."*

John 4:10

We have several big water troughs around our property
that we keep filled with good, clean water. We routinely clean
the troughs to keep algae out, we filter out the debris, and
we keep the water crystal clear for the horses to drink. We do
this because we know clean water is essential for horses to live
long healthy lives. We don't want them slurping in parasites or
bacteria with their life-sustaining water, so we make sure they
have good sources from which to drink.

A few of our horses, however, are a bit stubborn. There is a
mud puddle that forms near one of the gates after hard rains,
and instead of taking the few extra steps to the water troughs,
they will lean down and take a drink from that dirty water. It
is frustrating to see them do that, knowing that good clean
water is just a few steps away. But there they are, noses in the
mud, slurping up that dirt-tinged liquid.

Jesus reached out to the outcast woman in our passage today.

If she only knew the gift of God and who it was that was talking to her. She was having a conversation with God Himself, but she didn't realize it. He was offering her a life of so much more than her wayward heart could give. The passage continues in John 4 and tells us that she debated with Him about religion and politics, but He brought it back to her need for clean, living water—the gift of salvation and cleansing from sin that only He could give her. A heart sustained by a living relationship with Him.

We might need to take some time to evaluate. We may be drinking at the world's mud puddles instead of at God's water troughs. The world's puddles leave us with a dirty taste in our mouths and a dread in our hearts. We are outcasts, just as this woman was, but God offers us new living water; life restored by His grace through His great sacrifice and resurrection into new life through His power. Maybe we have been drinking from God's troughs, deeply quenching that soul thirst for love and acceptance that only comes through Him. If not, we should take those steps to the water trough of grace and quit drinking from the world's dirty puddles.

Thought-provoker:

Are we drinking the living water God offers through relationship with Him, or are we drinking the world's dirty water that never satisfies? What does living water look like in our lives?

Dear Lord, thank You for the troughs of living water that You offer. Help us to refuse the world's mud puddles that will never satisfy and help us to drink deeply from the love and grace You offer, for You are the only One who can truly satisfy our souls. In Jesus' name, Amen.

Notes/Insights:

New Pasture

Therefore, if anyone is in Christ, he is a new creation; old things have passed away; behold, all things have become new.

2 Corinthians 5:17

When we first moved to the farm, we only had one pasture for all the horses to graze. We kept them on that pasture as we prepared a new, bigger area for them to eat, move, and play. We wanted them to have the best grass and the bigger open field to spread out.

The issue that I had was when I opened the gate to the new pasture, the horses didn't want to go through. They were content to stay in the pasture that was familiar. Even though their current pasture's grass was scarce, they wouldn't budge. The new pasture awaited, but they wouldn't go through the gate. I literally had to prod them to go to the greener pasture because they didn't want to change. They seemed to think that different was automatically scary or bad.

I understand that horses don't have the reasoning skills to realize that I wouldn't put them in a pasture where I thought they would be in danger. I was patient with them, but I did push them to go out and try the new grass. Once they got a taste of the new grass, they forgot about the old pasture and looked forward to being in the new field. Once one horse got into the new field, he raised his head with his mouth full of grass and whinnied to the others to come join him.

Before we came to know Christ, we were sitting in a scarce pasture. The world cannot offer the love, mercy, grace and so many other blessings that the new pasture of the Christian life holds. Many of us were hesitant to step through the gate and accept the new life He has to offer. But now that we are here, we wonder how we could have ever thought this pasture was bad or scary. Once we tasted the new life in Christ, we don't ever need to go back to the scarcity the world has to offer.

And we need to remember that although we know the blessings, others are still hesitant. They see the lush green grass of a new life in Christ, but they are scared to walk through that gate. We need to patiently encourage them to come on in. We can be like that first horse, with his mouth full of grass, whinnying encouragement to them to come join us and find that this pasture is full of the blessings and nourishment God intended for His children, and we need to invite as many as we can to come join us.

THOUGHT-PROVOKER:

Are we excited about the new life we have in Christ? Are we sharing it with others by encouraging them to join in?

Dear Lord, thank You that new life in You is complete and fulfilling. Help us to live in the pasture of Your blessings and encourage many others to join in. In Jesus' name, Amen.

Notes/Insights:

THE STUMBLE

There is no fear in love; but perfect love casts out fear,
because fear involves torment. But he who fears has not been
made perfect in love. We love Him because He first loved us.
1 John 4:18–19

While enjoying one day out trail riding with my daughter, we were moving along the edge of the woods in a field. We were talking, moving at a leisurely pace, feeling the sun's warmth, and enjoying the day. The horses had been in good spirits, and they hadn't been spooked or been by the birds or the deer we had seen along the way. It was a beautiful day. Then it happened.

Suddenly, without warning, my horse went down. I was able to pull my feet out of the stirrups just before we hit the ground, and I jumped off as soon as the ground was under my feet. I spun around to face him, worried that he was having a medical emergency. As we investigated, we found that his hind foot had bogged in some unseen mud, he had tried to over-correct, and his feet had gotten tangled. I got him back on his feet, and there didn't seem to be any other signs of injury. The fear in his eyes, though, was very unsettling.

I think he was scared that I was going to punish him. That I would not trust him going forward but would always remind him of this moment. Instead of being angry, I stroked his neck and talked quietly to him. I wasn't angry with him; he is my back-pocket buddy. Even when he stumbled and fell, he is still mine, and I still love him as my horse. Nothing changes that.

Fear. We have all experienced it in some way or another. We let God down. We stumbled. We sinned. We wait in the torment of what we think He will do next. We think there will be only distrust and shame in our future because of what we did in the present. Instead of coming down hard on us, His love casts out the fear. He reassures us that even when we have failed, when we have fallen, we are still His. And what relief fills our hearts when we realize just how gracious He is.

In the days after the stumble, I made sure my horse knew that he was still loved and trusted. We went riding a few days later, and we had the best trail ride we had had in a long time. God does the same for us. When we have fallen and we are fearful, He comes to us with love. We get back up with the gift of forgiveness, and we love Him even more.

THOUGHT-PROVOKER:

Where have we fallen and are fearful in our lives? What does God want to restore with His love in us today?

Dear Lord, thank You that You are not a fickle God, but that You love us unconditionally. Help us to walk with You, accept Your grace, and love You more each day because of Who You are. In Jesus' name, Amen.

NOTES/INSIGHTS:

Big Mama

*But Jesus called them to them and said, "Let the little children
come to Me, and do not forbid them; for of such is the kingdom
of God. Assuredly, I say to you, whoever does not receive the
kingdom of God as a little child will by no means enter it."*

Luke 18:16–17

We are fortunate that our county has a Mounted Patrol
unit within the Sheriff's department. When my daughter started
taking horse lessons several years ago, the Mounted Patrol was
boarded at the barn where the lessons took place, and we got to
know the officers and the horses. We have kept in touch with
the Mounted Patrol through the years, and they have always
been willing to come talk to our 4-H group, give demonstrations, and walk the parades with us, as well as provide
protection and support in our community.

One of the horses they have is named Big Mama. A beautiful
Percheron draft cross, all black with long feathers on her feet and
a thick, bushy tail. She is eighteen hands tall, all muscle and a
force to be reckoned with if you find yourself on the wrong side of
the law. She can be very intimidating when she flares her nostrils
and moves toward you with her huge hooves and strong legs.

But Big Mama has another side. She loves kids. When Big Mama comes for demonstrations and community outreach, she loves to be pet and brushed, and she will bend her head toward any small child to see them with her kind eyes and nicker to put them at ease. She wants children to be comfortable around her. She is a great ambassador as children respond well to her gentleness, and she gives the officers an opportunity to build great rapport in the community.

Big Mama is a reminder that our awesome, Almighty God can handle the universe, and He still loves children. When Jesus walked this earth, He took time for the children. In fact, he told the adults to let the children come to Him. He responds to children with love and gentleness, and He wants them to be a part of His family. He reminds us that it is child-like faith that allows us to enter His kingdom.

We need to remember to be like Big Mama, to be like Jesus— to take time for the children and not to push them away from trusting Him. Big Mama helps children to bridge the gap of trust by being kind. She is huge, but gentle. Jesus is God, and yet He takes time for children. He has enough love for every single one of them. Let's spread that love to them today.

THOUGHT-PROVOKER:

Where are we sharing the love of Christ with children in our lives? Where do we need to adjust our lives so that we are not forbidding them to come to Him?

Dear Lord, thank You that You love the children. Help us to share Your love with them with gentleness and kindness so we can help them to come to You and become a part of Your kingdom. In Jesus' name, Amen.

Notes/Insights:

ROCKET AND ARAMIS

For by one Spirit we were all baptized into one body—whether Jews or Greeks, whether slaves or free—and have all been made to drink into one Spirit. For in fact the body is not one member but many.

1 Corinthians 12:13–14

They couldn't be more different. Rocket is a tall, black walking horse, with a Roman nose covered by a blaze. Aramis is a white and gray speckled Arabian with a gorgeous mane and long flowing tail. Rocket is somewhat stubborn, but a great horse for beginners and non-experienced riders. Aramis needs someone with a steady hand who knows how to ride. Rocket tends to be somewhat pushy at the gate, Aramis waits his turn. Rocket loves quiet trail rides away from the crowds; Aramis loves the parades where kids point and "ooh" and "aah" over his gorgeous features. Rocket is shoulder strong, Aramis pushes from behind. Two horses who could not be any more different, and yet they get along. They grew to be the best of companions because of Tonya.

Tonya loves them both. She purchased both of them at different times and from different places, and the two of them were brought together at the barn. Tonya worked with them, she fed them, cared for them, and kept them together so they could learn to get along. Two horses with very different looks, backgrounds, and personalities. And they became friends.

Many of us in the church are very different from each other. We have different nationalities, ethnicities, and backgrounds. There are cultural differences, food preferences, outlooks, and perspectives. Some of us prefer to be in small groups or away from the crowds, and others thrive on being in a large group with lots of interaction. Some are experienced and steady, others are new and enthusiastic. We couldn't be more different. And yet, because of Christ, we can get along. He loves all of us, purchased each of us from the darkness of sin and death, and gave us new life in His church. He cares for each of us, and He wants us to get along (John 17). He wants us to show the world that differences don't divide, they bring us together. We learn from each other, and we accept one another, just as Rocket and Aramis did. We can be the unlikely duets, the surprising friendships, and the contradictory companions that confound the world and prove that Christ's love rises above all our differences and brings us together.

Tʜᴏᴜɢʜᴛ-ᴘʀᴏᴠᴏᴋᴇʀ:

Are we living in division or are we loving our differences? How can we allow the love of Christ within the church to show the world how unity looks? How can we come together so we are different without being divided?

Dear Lord, thank You that You have one church, one family, made up of many people with different personalities, backgrounds and lives. We are all a part of Your family because of You. Help us be a unified body, moving forward to further Your kingdom. In Jesus' name, Amen.

NOTES/INSIGHTS:

THE NEW RUG

Therefore, if anyone cleanses himself from the latter, he will be a vessel for honor, sanctified and useful for the Master, prepared for every good work. Flee also youthful lusts; but pursue righteousness, faith, love, peace with those who call on the Lord out of a pure heart.

2 Timothy 2:21–22

While I do spend a lot of my time out at the barn, it's not the only place I dwell. We have a cozy farmhouse, and inside I have an office in which I write. I recently got a new rug. It grounds my desk in the small space and brightens up the room. It is a blue and cream floral pattern, and my favorite part is how soft it feels under my feet when I am working at my desk.

Our dog, Ava, has developed a sensitive stomach as she has gotten older. We have to be careful to keep her on a special diet and not let her get human food. We don't deliberately give her things she shouldn't have, but sometimes she finds things that have slipped to the floor, and they cause her digestive discomfort.

At five thirty this morning, her discomfort became my cleaning project. She discarded her tummy contents onto my new rug in the office. The noise woke me, and I immediately went to care for her—and my rug. Once I knew she was okay, I tackled cleaning the rug. It didn't take long to remove the stain because I started on it right after it happened, and I used the cleaner the manufacturer recommended. After a few minutes, the stain was gone.

What if we were as diligent about the stains of sin and pursuing cleanliness in our spiritual lives as I was about that rug? What a difference it would make in our lives and testimonies if we took sanctifying our souls as seriously as we do keeping the physical things nice in our homes. The Creator has told us what to do when a sin-stain happens. *If we confess our sins, He is faithful and just to forgive us our sins and to cleanse us from all unrighteousness,* (1 John 1:9). We would be wise to go to Him as soon as we recognize the stain sin has made and let Him cleanse us.

Another product I use on my rug is a stain inhibitor. It protects the fibers from being stained when things happen. Our passage today tells us to flee youthful lusts and pursue righteousness, faith, love, and peace. When we do this, we help to keep sin from staining the carpet of our testimony. After all, nobody wants a dirty carpet in their life's office. Thankfully, our dog showed me the importance of tackling the stains and applying inhibitor to help keep them from happening in the first place. May we be diligent in doing the same in our hearts and lives today.

THOUGHT-PROVOKER:

Are we living and growing in the sin-inhibitors of righteousness, faith, love, and peace? Where do we need to apply confession for forgiveness and cleansing today?

Dear Lord, thank You for the reminder to keep the rug clean in our hearts and lives today. Help us to apply both confession and sanctification as we walk with You today. In Jesus' name, Amen.

NOTES/INSIGHTS:

THE VIEW

"Let not your heart be troubled; you believe in God, believe also in Me. In My Father's house are many mansions; if it were not so, I would have told you. I go to prepare a place for you. And if I go and prepare a place for you, I will come again and receive you to Myself; that where I am, there you may be also."

John 14:1–3

Today, I am standing at the barn door once again looking at the view. As we have walked through the barn, learned the lessons around the barnyard and taken in new insights, I have enjoyed sharing with you. It has been my humble privilege to share the things God has shown me from our farm, and I hope that you have been able to see the truths from His Word as we saw these things together. As our journey comes to an end, I want to take a moment and look out.

From the barn door, I can see my neighbor's house; I see a barn cat sprawled out on top of a large rock sunning herself in the pasture; I see the trees and the blue sky. My gaze is pulled upward as I watch a few clouds floating in the sky, and I think about the eternal view we are going to see one day. That golden road that leads us past the Tree of Life and into the presence of Jesus Himself. That beautiful place, untarnished by sin and evil; the throne room where we will cast our crowns at His feet and give Him praise for all eternity. I cannot wait for that view to become our reality.

But I also turn my eyes toward the barn's hallway. I see the stalls that need to be cleaned, the hay that needs to be stacked, the tack that needs to be cleaned and repaired. While I wait on that eternal view, I have work to do. So do you.

We have friends and loved ones that need to be encouraged to come into God's pasture. We know those who are sick or suffering that need our prayers. We need to build each other up. We have relationships that need forgiveness breathed into them, and others that continue to deepen and grow our love with each passing day. We have joys yet to come.

THOUGHT-PROVOKER:

As we leave this journey to go on to the next one God has for us, let us remember that the view from the barn door is two-fold—there is a promise to come, and there is work to be done. And in it all, we have a Savior who loves us so very much that He walks with us every step of the way. We also have each other to shoulder the loads, to find laughter, to shed tears, and to walk this together to show the world that the view from the Barn Door is good, because He is good.

Dear Lord, thank You for this journey through the barnyard. Thank You that You are the Door to eternal life, and that You hold Your arms open wide to welcome all of us. Give us the strength to do the work and renew us with the hope of the eternal view You provide. In Jesus' name, Amen.

Notes/Insights:

ACKNOWLEDGEMENTS

This sixth book of the *Devotion from Everyday Things* series came about because of those who believed God was not yet finished with what needed to be shared. *Devotions from the Barn Door* was a team effort, and I want to thank those who have walked this journey with me.

To my family, who have continued to encourage me to write and allow me to share our stories, thank you. John, thank you for being the Godly husband that has allowed me to pursue this ministry. Thank you all for your support, your nudging, and your proof-reading skills. Each page is a reminder of how you all have encouraged me to keep going. Love you all.

To my Lighthouse family, thank you for your support and for allowing me to share your lives in my writings. You are the prayer warriors and exhorters who pulled me through the spiritual battles to get this written. You are an amazing community of believers, and my heart is grateful for all the prayers and encouragement.

To my friends—you still put up with me, listen to me bounce crazy ideas around, make me laugh, and love me no matter what—I love you all to the barn and back! To Cindie, who started all of this with a simple email, I cannot thank you enough for believing I could be an author. To Jennifer, this has not been an easy journey this time, but we have walked it together. Thank you.

To Mike and Paula Parker and the WordCrafts Press team—thank you for believing there was still another book in this series to be written. Your professionalism, confidence, and support through this past decade have been invaluable and only eternity knows what kind of impact your investment has been.

And to my heavenly Father, who has done more than I could have thought or imagined with a woman and a keyboard, thank You. To You be all the glory and honor.

About the Author

Tammy Chandler is a wife, mother, grandmother, teacher, friend, author, and public speaker. She accepted Christ as Savior when she was five years old, dedicated her life to full-time service as a teenager, and has worked in various ministries throughout her lifetime. She has a Bachelor of Education from Clearwater Christian College, and a Master of Education from Jones International University.

After many years of using everyday objects to teach children and teenagers, God allowed her to write *Devotions from Everyday Things* (Westbow Press), its follow-up, *More Devotions from Everyday Things*, *Devotions from Everyday Things: Horse & Farm Edition*, *Devotions from Everyday Jobs*, *Devotions from Everyday Sports*, and now, *Devotions from the Barn Door* to include a larger audience. She also co-wrote *Deployed with My Mother*, the true story of David Weill and his single mother as they both went to war in the desert.

When she is not writing, Tammy enjoys spending time with her husband, John, their grown children and their spouses, and the grandchildren. She still enjoys working the farm, riding the horses, and taking walks with their dog, Ava. They Chandlers live in Tennessee.

You can visit Tammy online at:
www.simplydevotions.wordpress.com

Also Available From

WordCrafts Press

In the Boat with Jesus
Marian Rizzo

Illuminations
Paula K. Parker & Tracy H. Sugg

Donkey Tales
Keith Alexis

Learning as I Go
Christy Bass Adams

Morning Mist
Barbie Loflin

www.WordCrafts.net

www.ingramcontent.com/pod-product-compliance
Lightning Source LLC
Chambersburg PA
CBHW021628120626
46545CB00002B/456